PAINT YOUR HOME

A READER'S DIGEST BOOK

Created and produced by De Agostini Editions
Interpark House
7 Down Street
London W1Y 7DS

Publishing Director: Frances Gertler
Art Director: Tim Foster
Senior Editors: Michèle Byam, Louise Tucker
Art Editor: Paul Tilby
Illustrations: Grundy & Northedge
Photographers: Geoff Dann, Tim Imrie, Matthew Ward

The credits and acknowledgements that appear
on page 136 are hereby made a part of this copyright
page.

Library of Congress Cataloging in Publication Data

Donegan, Francis.
        Paint your home: skills, techniques, and
tricks of the trade for professional looking interior
painting/Francis Donegan.
        p.   cm.
Includes index.
ISBN 0-89577-838-6
1. House painting—Amateurs' manuals. I. Title.
TT323.D66 1997
698'.14—dc21   96-46950

Printed in Spain

Warning
All do-it-yourself activities involve a
degree of risk. Skills, materials, tools,
and site conditions vary widely. Although
the editors have made every effort to
ensure accuracy, the reader remains
responsible for the selection and use of
tools, materials, and methods. Always
obey local codes and laws, follow
manufacturers' instructions,
and observe safety precautions.

PAINT YOUR HOME

**SKILLS, TECHNIQUES, AND TRICKS OF THE TRADE
FOR PROFESSIONAL LOOKING
INTERIOR PAINTING**

Reader's
Digest

THE READER'S DIGEST ASSOCIATION, INC.
PLEASANTVILLE, NEW YORK/MONTREAL

Contents

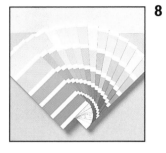
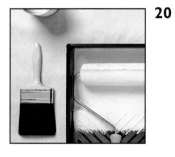

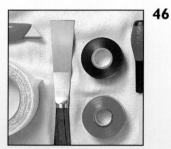
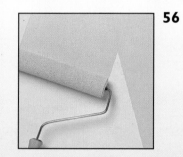

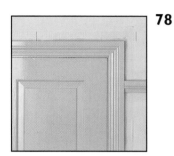

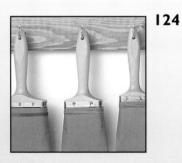

Introduction

Painting is the perfect project for the do-it-your-selfer. The beginner can quickly master the basic skills; professional-quality tools are readily available; and, once completed, the results are there for others to praise, and for you to enjoy.

Paint Your Home will help you to experience that enjoyment for yourself. How often have you had an idea for a painting project, but did not know where or how to begin? Now, you have a book which can guide you through the first planning stages, and on towards learning proper techniques of painting. More than that, it helps you to judge the quality of tools and equipment; and by working at your own pace, you will soon build up confidence in your ability.

The book is structured like a painting project. There are sections on planning, tools and materials, easy-to follow painting instructions accompanied by clear, precise illustrations, and tips on cleanup. Each chapter of *Paint Your Home* covers a different aspect of painting and builds on the information in the previous chapter. It is best to read the chapters in sequence so that you do not miss any important part of the project, or any of the tips and shortcuts that are scattered throughout the text. All this should help you to do a better job. It may even cut your working time, or save you money.

The book begins with a guide to help you select the right color or combination of colors for your project. This straightforward, practical approach will take the uncertainty out of selection, and will also make the job much easier and more enjoyable. We will show you how to combine colors by describing how the color wheel works. To achieve the perfect effect in a room, we will explain how you can use paint color to create a mood, and highlight or hide any features in the room.

By choosing the most suitable type of paint and the tools for your project, you can be assured of getting the perfect finish. The book also answers your technical queries. For instance, it will describe what substances go into a can of paint, and it will explain the differences between types of paint, and tell you which paint suits which job. And because the right tools could make your project so much easier and quicker, *Paint Your Home* offers a guide to the tools and equipment you need; as well as tips on how to judge the quality of these items.

Painting techniques and preparation form the heart of *Paint Your Home*. Using clear instructions and illustrations, it will show the correct way to hold and use a brush, roller or another applicator. Once you have mastered these techniques, you will be able to tackle any paint project with confidence.

And to help you achieve that 'professional look' to your finish, *Paint Your Home* shows you how to prepare the room properly in the first place. This section includes several chapters which tell you how to prepare the different sorts of surface that apply to different projects — such as walls, ceilings, or special situations, such as kitchen cabinets. Then illustrated step-by-step instructions will guide you through the best sequence for painting tasks.

At the end of every job there is inevitably some cleaning up to do, so *Paint Your Home* concludes by dispensing useful advice on how to clean and store tools and equipment. There are clear methods for disposing of used paint and solvents, as well as for safely storing unused materials.

Paint Your Home makes paint and painting easy to understand. The book will guide you through every stage of the process. Just follow the straightforward instructions and advice, and you will be able to enjoy the rewarding experience of painting your own home with professional-looking results.

FRANCIS DONEGAN

CHAPTER I

COLOR

The paint colors that you choose for the walls, ceiling, and floor in each room of your home make an important decorating statement. Paint colors not only reflect your personal tastes but also establish the character of your home. Because colors affect how you feel when you are in a room, they may be used to create a mood. Moreover, colors can be selected and combined to influence how you and others perceive the physical dimensions of a room.

Choosing color

There are thousands of paint colors to choose from, and each year manufacturers introduce dozens more. Begin the process of choosing your colors by deciding which you like best. Then consider what the room will be used for and what overall effect you wish to create. Paint color can be used to alter the spatial proportions of a room, highlight features, and detract from flaws. Other important factors to consider include the room's lighting and existing furnishings. This chapter will help you to combine your personal color preferences with the needs of the space to be painted. This knowledge will enable you to avoid mistakes. The main considerations are:

Understanding color It is important to understand how colors are created and how they work with one another. The color wheel is a useful device for understanding color, and it can help to make selecting color combinations easier. The color wheel is also useful for matching paints with furnishings, woodwork, and other elements in the room.

Creating an effect Consider what the room will be used for when you decide on the effect you wish to create. Rooms can evoke different moods: the feeling of a cozy bedroom is different from the mood of a large family room. The paint colors you select will help to create the mood. Also, colors can change the perceived dimensions of a space, making small rooms feel larger or large spaces more intimate.

Taking cues from the room You can use paint to hide any faults in a room, such as a run of pipes. By the same token, you can use color to highlight an architectural element or other feature. The light in a room also plays a part in color selection. Be sure to consider both natural and artificial light sources.

Dealing with your furnishings The colors of walls, ceilings, and floors cannot be considered in isolation. Rooms contain furniture, fittings, carpets, and pictures, and the colors you select should work well with whatever is in the room.

Planning your work Before you start a painting project, you should make sure that you have the correct color and quantity of paint. You should estimate how long the job will take and whether you will need to hire a contractor for some of the work.

COLOR TRENDS

Paint colors fall in and out of favor, as other products do. Fortunately, paint-color cycles usually last for seven to ten years rather than the one- or two-year cycles of fashion colors. When changes do occur, they tend to be gradual. So the colors you choose for your walls today will not be out-of-date next year.

The current paint-color trend is for warm colors, inspired by nature. Even cool colors, such as blues and greens, are being made warmer with the addition of yellow. The colors tend to be pale, especially when used over large surfaces. You can enliven a pale, warm scheme by adding bright accent colors.

Understanding color

The human eye can distinguish about 10 million different colors. Virtually all are derived from just three primary colors—red, blue, and yellow. The primary colors are combined in different concentrations, with white or black added to the mix. Red, blue, and yellow cannot be created by mixing other colors.

The color wheel The color wheel is a simple design device that can help you to choose colors and combinations of colors. The wheel features the three primary colors positioned equidistantly around the circle. Between each of these colors are the secondary colors—orange, green, and violet—created by mixing the two primary colors on either side. Tertiary colors are created by mixing a secondary color with a primary color. Colors can be mixed with one another in an almost limitless number of combinations to create new colors. Tints are created by adding white to colors. Adding black creates darker versions of colors, called shades.

The position of colors on the color wheel can help you to combine paint colors in the home. Complementary colors, which lie directly across from each other on the wheel, and related colors, which are positioned side by side on the wheel, usually yield the most successful combinations.

COLOR TERMS

Three words are often used when describing colors: hue, value, and intensity. These terms help to describe paint colors more precisely.

- **Hue** is simply the name of the color family to which a color belongs. For example, the hue of a ruby-colored vase is red.
- **Value** describes the relative lightness or darkness of a color. Light colors have a higher value than dark colors. For example, lemon yellow has a higher value than deep gold. *Tone* is a term that is often used interchangeably with *value*.
- **Intensity** describes how saturated with pigment a color is — in fact, intensity is often called saturation. A highly saturated, or intense, color will seem bright, not subdued.

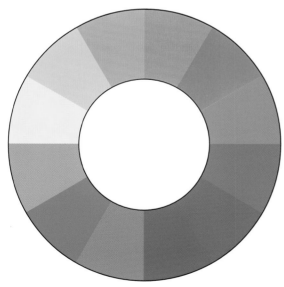

The color wheel
This simple color wheel shows the three primary colors, the three secondary colors, and the six tertiary colors. Mixing these 12 colors with one another, and with black and white, will create every other color it is possible to produce.

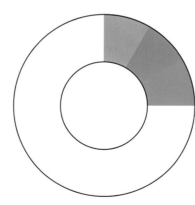

Related colors
Related colors are positioned next to one another on the color wheel. As they are made by mixing elements of each color, related colors blend together and do not clash. Any group of related colors used in a room will create a harmonious scheme.

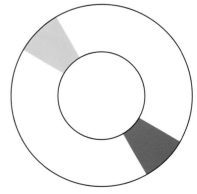

Complementary colors
Complementary colors lie directly opposite each other on the color wheel. When two complementary colors are used together in a room, each will provide a contrast for the other. They can be used to create attractive, dramatic color schemes.

The properties of colors As you work with complementary and related colors, take into account other principles that affect how colors work. Consider such factors as warm and cool colors, light and dark colors, and neutral colors before choosing paint colors.

Warm and cool colors

Warm colors are grouped together on the color wheel—they contain elements of yellow and red. Warm colors can make a surface appear to advance and a room seem small and intimate. Cool colors contain elements of blue and green, making a surface appear to recede from the viewer and a room seem larger. The room on the left is painted in a warm peach color, and it seems more intimate and smaller than the cool blue-green room on the right.

Light and dark colors

A light-colored surface reflects more light than a dark-colored surface. Consequently, rooms that are painted in a light color will appear more open and larger than they really are. Even a warm color can have this effect if there is sufficient white in the color used. Dark colors absorb light, define spaces, and make a room appear smaller. So the pale blue room on the left seems larger than the dark blue room on the right.

Neutral colors

Neutral colors—black, white, and gray—do not appear on the color wheel. Other colors with a great deal of white or black are also called neutrals, such as beige and cream. Neutral colors can provide the backdrop for other colors in a color scheme, or they can be used alone, as in the room shown here, to create a harmonious scheme.

COLOR-MIXING TIPS

- Colors appear more intense when set on a white or near-white background.
- Dark colors look even darker when placed near light colors.
- Complementary colors appear more intense when used next to each other.

Creating an effect

Colors can be used to establish certain moods and to alter our perception of space. Consider what the room will be used for when deciding on colors. You can create the required effect by combining colors following the principles of complementary and related colors, warm and cool colors, and light and dark colors *(see pp.10–11).*

Creating a mood As a rule, warm colors create a cozy, intimate mood and cool colors, a tranquil one *(p.11)*. However, you can combine colors to produce other effects. For instance, red details in a blue room will make the cool, tranquil room feel warmer, and both colors will appear more vibrant. The lightness and darkness of colors can affect mood, too. Deep yellow will produce a more intimate feeling than will pale lemon.

Creating spatial effects One of the most amazing aspects of color is the way it can visually change the shape and size of a room. The simplest example of this is painting a room with a light color. The walls will seem to recede, creating the impression of a larger space. Cool colors *(p.11)* will achieve the same effect. You can create the opposite effect by using dark or warm colors.

COLORS AND ARCHITECTURE

The architectural style of your house may help you to select paint colors. Many paint manufacturers have created color lines geared to specific styles of architecture, such as neoclassical, Victorian, and art deco. Others have developed paint collections that are meant to evoke the look of regional architecture, such as Mediterranean and Mexican. There are also palettes of color that suit more generic decorating styles, such as traditional or country.

These paint collections can be helpful because they pare down thousands of color choices to a more manageable number. All the paints in a palette share common characteristics, so if several are selected for one room, they should work well together.

CREATING MOODS

Cool, light, related colors
This room is painted in shades of cool blue and blue-green that create a relaxing, tranquil effect. The colors are light, making the room appear airy and open, and the walls tend to recede. As the colors in this room are all related, they create a unified scheme.

Warm, dark, complementary colors
This room appears warm and intimate because the deep-brick-color walls are dark and contain red. The walls tend to advance into the room. Sea-green woodwork complements the brick-color walls and adds impact to the scheme.

CREATING SPATIAL EFFECTS

Unifying interconnecting rooms
You can create an impression of unity and spaciousness in your home by painting rooms in related colors. The colors will lead the eye from one room to another and produce a harmonious effect.

Different walls, different colors
Make a long, narrow room seem wider by painting the short walls a warm, dark color so that they seem to advance. The long walls will appear to recede away from each other if you paint them in cool, pale colors.

Making a ceiling appear higher
Walls divided by a picture rail provide interesting challenges. Here the ceiling and the area above the rail are painted a lighter color than the area under the rail to give an illusion of spaciousness and a high ceiling.

Making a ceiling appear lower
This ceiling and the wall area above the picture rail are painted a darker color than the area under the rail. The visual effect is to lower the ceiling and to give the space a more intimate feeling.

Highlighting features and hiding faults

Paint color can enhance or camouflage elements in a room. Before you start painting, consider whether there are any features that should have impact or be hidden.

Highlighting features To enhance an architectural feature, such as a molding or a window frame, give it a paint treatment different from that of the surrounding area. You could use complementary colors *(p.10)*. These colors lie directly opposite each other on the color wheel, and when they are placed side by side, they tend to make each other stand out. An alternative strategy is to create contrast with light and dark colors. For example, dark green will stand out against pale yellow even though the two colors are near each other on the color wheel.

Hiding faults To help conceal a fault, such as an ugly radiator or pipes, make it blend in with the background. One way to do this is to paint the fault the same color as the wall surface surrounding it. Another way to disguise flaws is by using a flat paint sheen rather than a shiny finish.

HIDING FAULTS

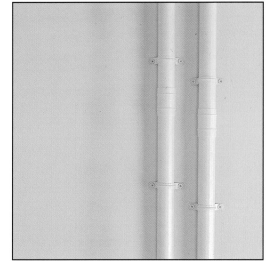

Pipes
These pipes have been painted the same color as the surrounding wall area. This helps to make them appear less noticeable.

HIGHLIGHTING FEATURES

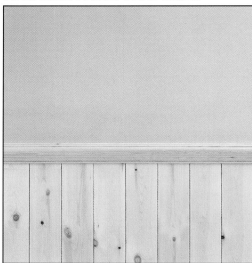

Walls and woodwork
Wood wainscoting that extends part of the way up a wall can be an attractive feature. The wainscoting here has been left natural, and the wall has been painted in lilac. This color complements the natural wood wainscoting and draws attention to it.

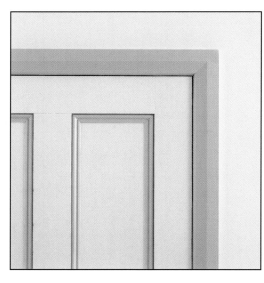

Door and door frame
This paneled door has been painted in two related colors. The related colors both emphasize the panels and, at the same time, establish a feeling of unity. The door frame has been painted in the same colors to harmonize with the door.

Crown molding
Crown molding can be a stunning architectural feature. This example is painted in a lighter color and with a shinier finish than the surrounding wall. Both features make the molding stand out in the room.

The effect of light

The type and intensity of light can change the appearance of a paint color. When you are selecting color, you should consider the natural light in a room and the type of artificial lights that you will use.

Natural light The quality of natural light in a room will affect colors. For example, bright colors seem brighter in direct sunlight. The natural light in a room will be governed by the time of day, the season, and the direction the room faces. Generally, natural light at noon has a blue cast, and at sunrise and sunset, it has an orange cast. The time of sunrise and sunset will change with the seasons, and light is brighter in summer than in winter. The direction a window faces will also determine when the room will have most natural light and whether it is direct or indirect light.

Artificial light The main types of artificial light used in homes are incandescent, fluorescent, and halogen light. Incandescent light has a yellow cast slightly deeper than that of sunlight. It works with darker, warmer colors. Fluorescent light contains blue and works with bright colors and white; it is often used in kitchens and bathrooms. Halogen light gives a strong white light that defines bold colors but can wash out muted hues.

HOW LIGHT AFFECTS COLORS

How natural light affects colors
The quality of natural light changes over the course of a day. This picture shows a room at noon when the natural light is brightest. The pale walls appear to have a slightly blue cast. A south-facing window will have direct light which is brighter than the indirect light of a north-facing window.

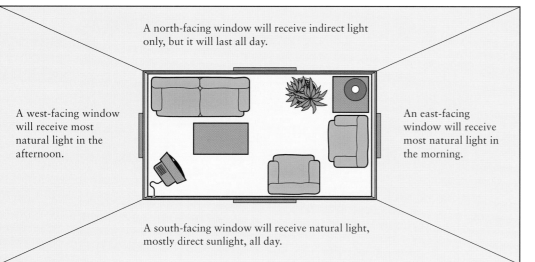

A north-facing window will receive indirect light only, but it will last all day.

A west-facing window will receive most natural light in the afternoon.

An east-facing window will receive most natural light in the morning.

A south-facing window will receive natural light, mostly direct sunlight, all day.

Get your bearings
The direction that a window faces affects when a room receives natural light and the type of light it receives. Light will shine through a window at different times of day, as the illustration above shows.

How artificial light affects colors
At night, all the light in a room will come from artificial sources. The light from incandescent bulbs has a yellow cast. This will tend to make a room seem warmer.

Using existing furnishings

It is essential to consider the dominant colors in the furnishings you already own or plan to add to the room when selecting paint colors. Just as the colors of walls and woodwork should work well together, so too should the painted surfaces harmonize with furniture, pictures, window treatments, floor coverings, and other elements in the room. In fact, purchasing new furniture or carpeting often calls for repainting the room.

Do you want your furniture to stand out or blend in with the colors of the walls and woodwork? Photographs or other works of art you intend to hang on the wall will also affect the color you select for the room. A busy, primary-colored art print will lose impact when hung on a brightly colored wall, but it is more likely to stand out against a neutral color scheme.

Houseplants will add green and natural wood will add brown to the color scheme of a room. Consider how much natural-wood furniture there is in the room and whether there is a wooden floor; the wood will add warmth to a room.

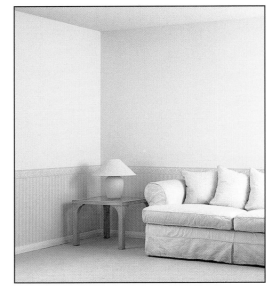

Paint and wallpaper
Paint has been used with wallpaper in this room. The wallpaper under the chair rail has pale and deep peach stripes, and the pale peach has been selected for the paint color above the rail. This creates a well-balanced scheme of related colors.

Brightly patterned sofa
This bright sofa in the complementary colors of blue and terracotta is the focal point in the room. The colors work well together because the walls have been painted the same deep terracotta as one of the less dominant colors in the sofa fabric.

Pale-patterned rug and curtains
The pale greens in the rug and curtains are all related colors. The walls have been painted a pale pink that complements pale green. This creates a harmonious scheme, drawing attention to the rug and curtains.

Houseplants in a warm-colored room
The houseplants in this room cool down the red walls. Green complements red, and each color seems more vibrant when placed next to the other. The sisal flooring provides a neutral ground for the wall colors.

Planning your painting project

Before beginning your painting project, be sure that you have planned each stage of work. This involves buying the paint, making sure that you have set aside enough time to complete the job, and hiring a contractor if necessary.

Buying the right color You can begin your quest for the perfect paint color by taking a sample of the color in any medium—it could be a swatch of fabric, a cutting from a magazine, or chips from a damaged wall painted in a color you want to replicate. The sample can be used to find a match in a paint manufacturer's range of standard colors or to have a paint custom-blended.

The most common method of selecting paint colors is to use manufacturers' paint chips. These are strips of paper that show incremental shades of a single color. You can use paint chips to check which color matches your sample most closely. Also, you can test which paint chips will work best with other colors in your home. Try several manufacturers' ranges because the colors vary in each collection. If you don't find the color you want among those in a range, you can have a paint specially custom-blended.

To request a custom-blended paint, use your sample or find a paint chip that most closely matches the hue you want. Then consult with the paint expert at your local outlet. Most experts will use a computer to analyze the color and blend a paint to match the sample. The challenge is to ensure that the custom-blended paint will match the sample after it is applied. Paint and fabric colors look different from each other because of the finish. If you use a fabric sample, the color of the painted surface will not appear to be exactly the same. Moreover, variations in sheen or texture may lead to a mismatch between the original sample and the end result. It is best to buy a quart of paint at first and to try the color out on a patch of the material you will be painting. Allow the paint to dry and judge the effect for about a week, in different parts of the room and in different light conditions.

COLORS BY COMPUTER

Many paint suppliers use computer matching to create custom-blended paint colors. The process is simple. You provide the computer operator with a flat color sample, usually at least ½ inch in diameter. Then the sample is placed in a device attached to the computer. The computer analyzes the color on the sample and breaks it down into its primary-color components. Then the computer produces a recipe for mixing a similar color of custom paint.

Depending on how complex the color is and how good the sample is, the computer should yield the right color. You should buy about a quart and test the color on sample boards. If the color is not suitable, you can have the store alter the formula slightly and blend a new color.

The service is free at some stores (it is included in the price of custom-blended paint), while other retailers charge a minimal fee, which is usually less than $10. The custom-blended paint will cost more than paint from a manufacturer's range, but it is a nearly certain way to obtain the right color.

WHITE PAINT

Buying white paint isn't as straightforward as you may think. Most companies offer a range of whites with names like Antique White, Linen White, Lilac White, and even Off-White. These are not pure white paints but contain small amounts of tinting. When shopping, make sure that the white you buy is the shade of paint you want.

BUYING THE RIGHT QUANTITY

To estimate the amount of paint you'll need, calculate the area of surface to be painted in each room. To measure the area of a ceiling, multiply the length by the width of the room. To calculate the area of a wall, multiply the length by the height. Calculate the area of all the walls by adding their square footage together. Be sure to include the additional area in any alcoves. Then calculate the area of all windows and doors by multiplying their height by their width. Standard windows are about 15 square feet, and doors are about 20 square feet. Then subtract the total area of all windows and doors from the total area of the walls. To calculate the area of molding, multiply the height by the length. For narrow trim, measure the sides and tops of windows and doors and add the totals together.

Next, multiply the area to be painted by the number of coats of paint you plan on applying. Divide that number by the surface area that a can of paint can cover. Most gallon cans state a coverage rate of 400 square feet when painting smooth interior walls. However, it is best to estimate that a can will cover only about 350 square feet so that you will have a little extra paint left over for touch-ups later.

CALCULATIONS AT A GLANCE

Ceiling area:
Length x width = __ sq. ft.

Wall area:
Length x height = __ sq. ft.

Door area/window area:
Height x width = __ sq. ft.

To calculate the surface area of all the walls in a room:
Total area of all the walls minus the total area of all the windows and doors in the room. = __ sq. ft.
(Total surface area)

To calculate the total area to be painted:
Total surface area x number of coats = __ sq. ft.
(Total area to be painted)

To calculate the number of gallon cans of paint to buy:
Total area to be painted ÷ area covered by a gallon of paint (approx. 350 sq. ft.) = __ gallon cans
(Total gallon cans needed)

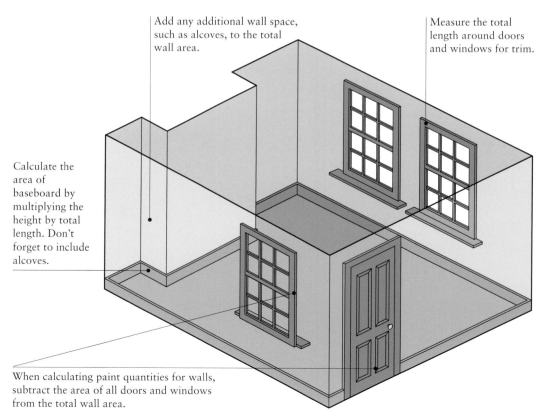

Add any additional wall space, such as alcoves, to the total wall area.

Measure the total length around doors and windows for trim.

Calculate the area of baseboard by multiplying the height by total length. Don't forget to include alcoves.

When calculating paint quantities for walls, subtract the area of all doors and windows from the total wall area.

Calculating the surface area of walls
Most rooms are not perfect rectangles. Measure the dimensions of each section of wall separately and calculate the area. You may have more than four wall areas to add together in order to calculate the total surface area of the walls in your room.

A QUESTION OF TIME

Home-improvement projects always take longer than you think they will, and painting is no exception. Professionals cover at least 400 square feet of wall surface with a roller in one hour. You may equal that rate in the first hour, but you are likely to tire and slow down. Preparation work, such as cutting in (*p.130*) and moving furniture, will take even longer.

Below is a practical schedule for painting a 10-by-20-foot living room. Adapt the schedule for your project:

Day 1 Buy your materials and supplies. If you are planning to start the project on a specific day, buy your materials an evening or two before the work will begin. Finding the right tools and paint may take longer than expected.

Day 2 Do all the preparation work. This is a time-consuming task that should be planned adequately. After preparation, set up for painting: move furniture, put down drop cloths, and so on.

Day 3 Paint in the right order. Plan your sequence of work. If you start early, you may be able to apply a second coat of water-based paint on the same day that you apply the first.

HIRING A CONTRACTOR

Although you will be able to paint your home yourself, you may wish to hire a contractor for a particularly difficult area or if time is at a premium. A contractor should do a good job and complete it quickly. Cost is the major drawback to hiring a contractor. As much as 80 percent of the cost of a typical paint project can be attributed to labor charges.

WHAT SHOULD BE IN EVERY CONTRACT

A contract between you and a professional should contain the following:

- The contractor's name, address, and phone number.
- The cost of the project.
- The scope of the project.
- Material specifications, such as the type of paint.
- Start and completion dates.
- Penalty clauses for work not completed on time. (Most painters will resist this, but try to include it.)
- The amount of deposit the contractor requires.
- A payment schedule. Don't pay the entire bill before the job is done. Withold 5–10% as a payment to be made at the completion of the job, once you are satisfied with the work.

CHECKLIST FOR HIRING A CONTRACTOR

- Gather names. Painting contractors are listed in the Yellow Pages and advertised in local newspapers. Check with people you know who have had similar work done. Generally, recommendations are more valuable than advertisements.
- Meet with three or four candidates. Discuss the project with each of them and ask them to tell you about how they prepare the surfaces, the types of paint they recommend, and how long the project will take. Ask to see a Certificate of Insurance, a document that verifies that the contracting company is insured.
- Ask for references. Contact people the contractor has worked for and ask questions about the contractor, such as: Was the final cost the same as the original estimate? Did he clean up properly?
- Ask for estimates. Supply each contractor with the same specifications and ask for an estimate of the cost of the job.
- Make a selection. When making your final decision, consider estimates, references, and how you think you will get along with the painter.
- Draw up a contract.

CHAPTER 2

MATERIALS AND TOOLS

One way to ensure the success of any painting project is to start with good-quality materials and tools. There are hundreds of paints available; this chapter will enable you to select the one that will work best on the surface you want to cover and protect. Complement premium paints by using the correct tools. They will make your work easier and will enable you to achieve the best results.

What's in paint?

Paints can be divided into two broad categories: water-based paints, such as acrylic and latex paints, and oil-based paints, such as alkyd paints. Within each group there are many different products. Some, such as primers and topcoats, are designed for specific tasks, and others, called specialty paints, are designed for specific conditions. Most paints contain the same basic ingredients—solvents, binders, pigments, and additives.

Although all paints are made from these same ingredients, the quality of the raw materials and the formulas used to blend them together make one paint different from another. For example, high-gloss paints contain a relatively high proportion of binder, which is left behind to form a protective layer on the surface when the solvent evaporates. On the other hand, flat paints, which give the dullest finish, contain a lower percentage of binder.

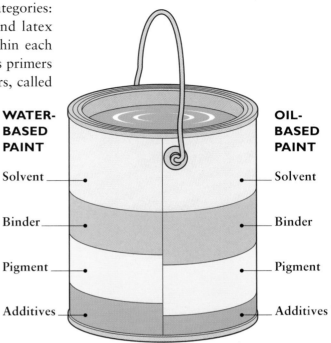

WATER-BASED PAINT   OIL-BASED PAINT

Solvent — Solvent

Binder — Binder

Pigment — Pigment

Additives — Additives

Solvent makes paint sufficiently fluid to apply easily. Water-based paints are so called because water is the solvent used. In oil-based paints, the solvent is either a mineral spirit, such as benzine, or a plant derivative, such as turpentine. As paint dries on a surface, the solvent in the paint evaporates, leaving only the solids (the binder and pigments). The solvents used in paints are the same materials that are used for the cleanup of solvent-thinned paints.

Binder makes paint stick to surfaces and develop a protective film. New binders are usually made from plastics. In water-based paints, the binder is usually an acrylic material or a combination of vinyl and acrylics. In oil-based paints, the binder is an oil-based product or a synthetic resin known as alkyd resin.

Pigment is made of finely ground particles that give paint its color and covering power. The particles tend to sink to the bottom of the can, which is why it is important for paint to be shaken or stirred before it is applied to a surface. Varnishes are unpigmented paint.

Some pigments are better than others. Prime pigments give the paint color and opacity. Extender pigments add bulk to the paint. Good-quality paints contain a high percentage of prime pigments.

Additives enhance paints in some way. Some additives make the paint easier to apply, some reduce mildew; others thicken paint to reduce the possibility of drips.

PROFESSIONAL TIP

The labels on paint cans provide important information. They usually tell you the type of paint, the name of the binder, the surfaces the paint can be applied to, and how much surface it will cover. The label may also give advice on how to prepare the surface you are about to paint. Also, the label will provide safety information, which you should read before you open the can.

Types of paint

While both water- and oil-based paint can be used on interior walls and woodwork, water-based paints have become the coatings of choice for most homeowners and many professional painters. There are three main reasons for this:

1 Water-based paints usually dry within a few hours. This means that you can apply two coats in the same day.

2 Brushes, rollers, and the painter can be cleaned with soap and water. Cleanup of oil-based paints requires the use of mineral spirits or turpentine, which are harsh solvents.

3 Compared with oil-based paints, water-based paints are relatively free of unpleasant odors and fumes. Oil-based paints also contain a higher amount of volatile organic compounds (*right*) than water-based paints do.

The long drying time of oil-based paints gives them a smooth finish: the longer the paint is wet, the more time it has to level out. This helps to eliminate brush marks, especially on wood.

VOCs AND PAINTS

Volatile organic compounds (VOCs) are a group of carbon-based chemicals, such as gasoline, alcohol, and paint thinner. They can damage lungs and form smog when they react with the atmosphere or sunlight. Oil-based paints contain the highest levels of VOCs, although a small amount can be found in water-based paints. Some states now regulate the use of VOCs in paint, and many manufacturers have reformulated their products to meet the regulations. For oil-based paints, this often means reducing the amount of solvent. This can make the paints more difficult to apply. For water-based paints, manufacturers must find substitutes for the additives that contain VOCs.

TYPES OF PAINT

General Types	Comments	Surfaces
Water-based paints	The most widely used type of paint for walls, ceilings, and woodwork, it does not normally require thinning and is easy to apply and clean up. All painters like water-based paints because they dry within a few hours. However, some people are sensitive to their odor.	Primed wood, wallboard, and plaster; surfaces previously painted with water-based paint.
Oil-based paints	Oil-based paints give a durable coating. Modern oil-based paints use a synthetic resin, or alkyd, as the binder, and they have largely replaced older-style paints that used linseed oil. Clean up with mineral spirits or turpentine.	Primed wood, wallboard, and plaster; any previously painted surface.
Specific-use paints		
Ceiling paints	These are thicker than standard water-based paints. They provide more coverage and tend to drip less than standard paints.	Ceilings.
Floor/deck paints	Designed to withstand the heavy wear floors are often subjected to, they are available in both water and oil bases. Some contain epoxy additives for increased adhesion.	Wood and concrete floors.
Textured paints	These are water-based paints that contain sand, styrofoam beads, or some other component that provides a rough, stuccolike texture. In addition, they can hide flaws in walls and ceilings.	Primarily wallboard ceilings, but can be used on other surfaces.
Kitchen and bathroom paints	A relatively new type of water-based paint that contains mildewcides to deal with the high humidity levels in kitchens and bathrooms.	Ceilings and walls.
Paint for children's rooms	A few manufacturers have introduced water-based paints designed for use in children's bedrooms and playrooms. These paints are easier to clean than other types. Some are also nontoxic.	Walls, ceilings, and woodwork.

PAINT SHEENS

It wasn't so long ago that the choice of sheens or the glossiness of paints was fairly limited. Every painter knew that flat paint was used on walls and that semigloss or high gloss was usually used on woodwork. But since the introduction of intermediate levels of gloss, these rules have changed.

The new finishes make it easier to match levels of paint sheen with surfaces. However, along with the new gloss levels came new names. Ranging from the dullest-looking finish to the shiniest, some of those you will encounter include flat, low-luster, eggshell, satin, soft gloss, semigloss, and high gloss. Bear in mind, though, that some of these names have slightly different meanings when you compare one brand of paint with another.

Sometimes you will see the word *enamel* linked with a sheen, such as semigloss enamel. Enamels contain materials that cause the paint to dry to a very hard finish.

Comparing paint sheens

Each level of paint sheen has different characteristics. Flat paints tend to absorb rather than reflect light, so they are good choices for hiding surface flaws. However, they are also more difficult to keep clean. High-gloss paints have the opposite qualities. They reflect light and appear very shiny. Since they are so smooth, dirt cannot stick to them as easily as it does to flat paint. This makes the surface much easier to clean. However, because these sheens accentuate imperfections on a surface, they are rarely used to cover entire walls.

Before selecting a sheen, consider the qualities of the surface, including the location and how much damage it may sustain. Then balance these against the characteristics of the sheen. Generally, you should cover walls with a flat or eggshell paint, and woodwork with a semigloss.

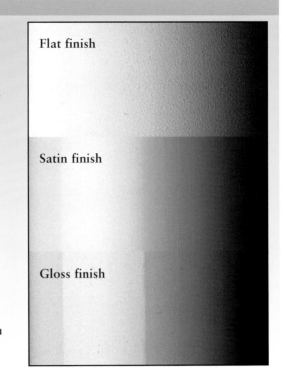

Flat finish

Satin finish

Gloss finish

MATCHING SHEEN TO SURFACE

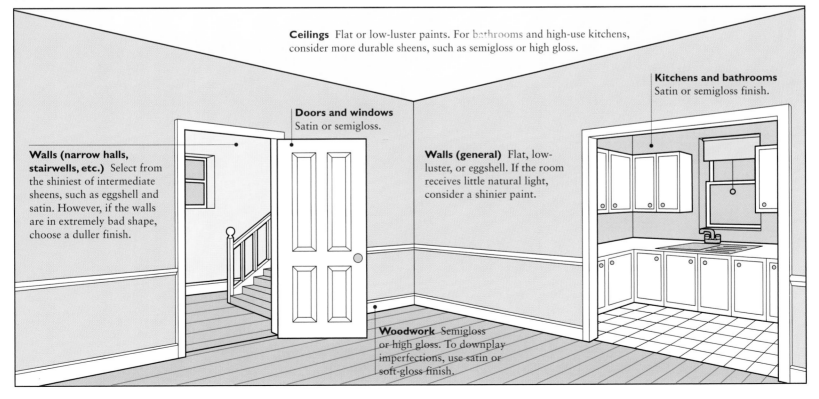

Ceilings Flat or low-luster paints. For bathrooms and high-use kitchens, consider more durable sheens, such as semigloss or high gloss.

Kitchens and bathrooms Satin or semigloss finish.

Doors and windows Satin or semigloss.

Walls (narrow halls, stairwells, etc.) Select from the shiniest of intermediate sheens, such as eggshell and satin. However, if the walls are in extremely bad shape, choose a duller finish.

Walls (general) Flat, low-luster, or eggshell. If the room receives little natural light, consider a shinier paint.

Woodwork Semigloss or high gloss. To downplay imperfections, use satin or soft-gloss finish.

Primers

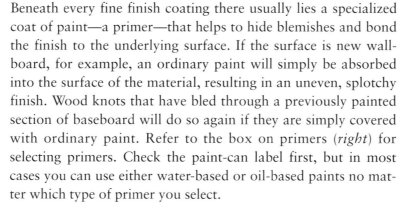

Beneath every fine finish coating there usually lies a specialized coat of paint—a primer—that helps to hide blemishes and bond the finish to the underlying surface. If the surface is new wallboard, for example, an ordinary paint will simply be absorbed into the surface of the material, resulting in an uneven, splotchy finish. Wood knots that have bled through a previously painted section of baseboard will do so again if they are simply covered with ordinary paint. Refer to the box on primers (*right*) for selecting primers. Check the paint-can label first, but in most cases you can use either water-based or oil-based paints no matter which type of primer you select.

Most primers are paints that contain very little pigment, but they are able to adhere to the surfaces they are designed to cover and to provide a good base for the paint.

Primers tend to dry more quickly than most paints (*p.25*). This means that you can usually prime and top-coat a surface in the same day. However, be aware that primers should not be left exposed for long periods. They do not contain many of the ingredients that make finish coatings durable and weather-resistant. If you wait too long, you will have to apply another coat of primer. Check the label for recommendations on timing.

Like paints, primers are available in both water and oil bases. Most are white, but you can tint them or ask your paint dealer to tint the primer to resemble the color that you will be using on the top coat.

In addition to primers that are brushed or rolled on, spot primers are also available. These products often contain shellac and are available as a liquid or in spray cans. They come in handy for hiding wood knots, marker and crayon stains, and water stains that bleed through paint.

PRIMER ON PRIMERS

Surface to be painted	Recommended primer
Unpainted wallboard	Water-based primer.
Unpainted plaster	Water-based primer.
Unpainted wood	Oil- or water-based primer.
Wood knots, other stains	Oil-based primer.
Previously painted walls, ceilings, woodwork	Water-based, but choose oil-based if staining is present.
Repairs in drywall or plaster	Water-based primer.
Repairs in wood	Oil- or water-based primer.
Masonry surfaces	Primer designed for masonry surfaces. Both oil- and water-based available.
Metal surfaces	Primer designed for metal. There are bright-metal primers, to use where metal is new or rust has been removed, and rusty-metal primers, which inhibit rust.

SPECIALTY PAINTS

A number of paint products are designed for special uses. Read the directions carefully before using.

Type of paint	Comments	Where to use it
Epoxy Paints	These paints are for covering nonporous surfaces, such as ceramic tile and metal. Difficult for the amateur to apply correctly.	Nonporous materials: tile, metal, plastic.
Heat-Resistant Paints	These paints will not degrade under high temperatures, such as those found around the opening of a fireplace or the metal of a radiator.	Hearths, radiators, pipes, etc.
Vapor Retarder/ Sealer Paints	Some water- and all oil-based paints stop the transmission of water vapor. This is important if there is no vapor retarder in the walls of the house and one is recommended by local building practice.	Walls and ceilings. Good when used as a primer in bathrooms.

Stains and varnishes

In addition to paint, there are other types of coatings that can be used to enhance or protect wood features in your home. These include stains and clear-finish varnishes.

Stains are designed to color a surface yet allow the wood grain to show through. Unlike paints, which form a protective layer on a surface, stains are absorbed into the wood, but they must be covered by a clear protective finish—a varnish.

Varnishes are clear finishes that form a tough coating over stains. They can also be used over painted surfaces. Like paints, they are available in both water-based and oil-based versions. Polyurethanes are currently the most popular types of varnish, owing to their ease of application and great durability. Still, traditional spar varnish is often used where a flexible gloss finish is needed. And a large number of other new products have been developed to meet special needs. They are available in a range of finish sheens from satin to high gloss.

Combination products are so called because they contain both stain and varnish. Available in both water-based and oil-based versions, they can change the color of wood as well as provide it with a protective coating.

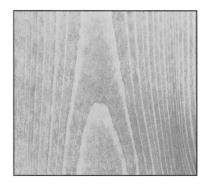

Transparent stains
With transparent stains, most of the wood grain shows through the finish, thereby enhancing the qualities of the wood.

Semitransparent stains
Semitransparent stains allow some wood grain to show through, but they are selected for their hiding ability.

Polyurethanes
These products are clear finishes designed to protect other finishes. Most commonly used on stained wood, they can also be applied over paints.

DRYING TIMES FOR PAINTS	
Types of paint	**Typical drying times***
Water-based primer	1–4 hours; recoat immediately.
Oil-based primer	4–10 hours; recoat after 24 hours.
Pigmented shellac	30 minutes to 1 hour; recoat immediately.
Water-based paint	2–4 hours; recoat immediately.
Oil-based paint	6–10 hours; recoat after 24 hours.
Water-based stain	2–4 hours; apply protective coat after 12–24 hours.
Oil-based stain	4–6 hours; apply protective coat after 24 hours.

Check paint-can label for specific drying and recoating times.

Brushes

Paintbrushes are divided into two categories: one is natural-bristle brushes, which are made from animal hair, and the other is synthetic-bristle brushes, which are made of nylon, polyester, or a combination of the two. As a general rule, use a synthetic-bristle brush for water-based paints and a natural-bristle brush for oil-based paints. You can also use a good-quality synthetic-bristle brush for oil-based paints, but never use natural bristles with water-based paints, as the bristles will absorb the water in the paint and the brush will be ruined. Many painters believe that the best natural-bristle brushes are China bristle, which means that boar's hair was used to make the brush. Among synthetic-bristle brushes, nylon and polyester do an equally good job.

Testing the quality of a new paintbrush Good paintbrushes have dense bristles. You should check that the metal ferrule is solid and well attached to the handle, which can be of wood or heavy plastic. The bristles of a good-quality brush should also be strongly anchored to the handle; the bristles of an inferior brush will come out in your hand. Set a "bargain" brush next to a more expensive one, and the difference will be clear.

THE RIGHT BRUSH FOR THE JOB	
Brush size	**Uses**
2-inch (straight and angled bristles)	Trim and windows
2½-inch	Trim and cutting in
3-inch	Doors, walls, and ceilings
4-inch	Walls and ceilings
Stencil brush	Corners and intricate moldings

2-inch brush

2-inch angled brush

2½-inch brush

Using new brushes Remove the wrapping and drag the brush back and forth across your palm, flexing the bristles slightly with your fingers. They should spring back into position when you release the pressure. Before painting, dip the brush in the appropriate solvent (water if you are using water-based paint, mineral spirits for oil-based paint) and remove the excess.

Refurbishing old brushes A brush that is stored properly won't have to be refurbished. However, if you neglected a favorite brush the last time you painted, follow these steps:

1 Soak the brush overnight in the appropriate solvent. If using mineral spirits, keep them away from open flames.
2 Use a brush comb to remove paint (*below right*).
3 Dry the brush by blotting on newspaper and waving it about.
4 Test the bristles by pulling them lightly and flexing them against a hard surface. If some of the bristles are still stuck together or, even worse, some fall out, invest in another brush.

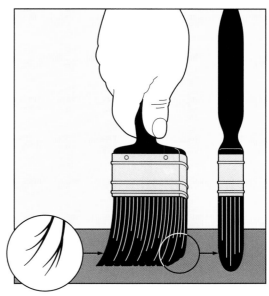

Choosing a good-quality brush
Bristles should be packed tightly on the brush, with no open spaces. They should be of different lengths so that they form a chiseled edge at the tip. Each bristle should have a frayed end to apply the paint smoothly and evenly.

3-inch brush

4-inch brush

Stencil brush

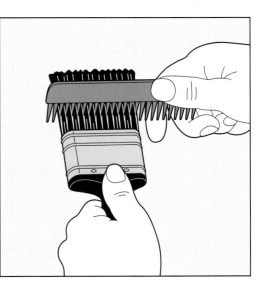

Using a brush comb
Plastic or metal brush combs and wire brushes can remove loosened paint without damaging the bristles.

Rollers

Rollers allow you to paint large open areas of walls, ceilings, and floors quickly and efficiently. Good-quality rollers have two sections: the frame, sometimes called the roller handle, and the cover, which is a napped cylinder that holds and applies the paint. Standard roller covers are 9 inches long, but you can find 18-inch rollers. Although the 18-inch size covers a larger area more quickly, it is heavier and more cumbersome to use and takes some getting used to. You will undoubtedly achieve better results with a 9-inch roller.

Using a new roller Remove the wrapping and smooth out the nap with your hand. Apply the appropriate solvent (p.30) and rub it into the nap. Remove excess solvent by squeezing the roller with your hand. Load the roller with paint and make a few practice passes on some scrap material before tackling a wall or ceiling.

Choosing a Roller Frame

The frame should have a cap at each end to prevent paint from collecting inside the cover and to allow it to roll smoothly. Squeeze the frame and check that the sides spring back into position when you ease the pressure. The handle of the roller frame should be rigid. The hand grip should be comfortable and have a hollow, threaded end to fit an extension pole for painting ceilings and high areas (p.70).

Roller Covers

Synthetic roller covers work well for water-based paints. For oil-based paints, use lamb's wool or mohair covers. The core of the cover should be made of plastic; cardboard cores degrade quickly and will not last.

TYPES OF ROLLER COVERS

Cover naps	Recommended surfaces
Short: 1/4-inch	Flat walls and ceilings.
Medium: 3/8- to 3/4-inch	Surfaces with small flaws and bumps.
Long: up to 11/4-inch	Textured surfaces.

Short: 1/4-inch nap   Medium: 3/4-inch nap   Long: 11/4-inch nap

Power rollers

These tools are designed to pump paint directly from the can or a special reservoir to the cover of a paint roller. Because you don't have to continually stop painting to load the roller, you can finish a job relatively quickly. Still, you must keep the roller moving to avoid drips and runs.

The typical power-roller kit will contain roller extensions, covers, a hose, a pump, and a reservoir or paint-can cover. Be sure the hose is long enough to make using a power roller worthwhile. If the hose is too short, you will have to keep moving the paint can or reservoir, which defeats the whole purpose of using this type of roller. Since it takes additional time both to set up a power roller and clean it at the end of the project, consider using this tool only for large projects.

Paint pads

These tools consist of a foam rubber painting surface and a plastic handle. They can be used to apply water-based paints and water-based varnishes. Harsh solvents, such as those found in paint removers, can actually melt the rubber.

Large paint pads allow you to work faster than you would be able to with a brush, although not as quickly as you can with a roller. However, pads are rarely used for large open areas because they tend to spread the paint too thinly, requiring an extra coat of paint. Smaller paint pads, though, can do a good job on narrow sections of trim, such as muntins on windows.

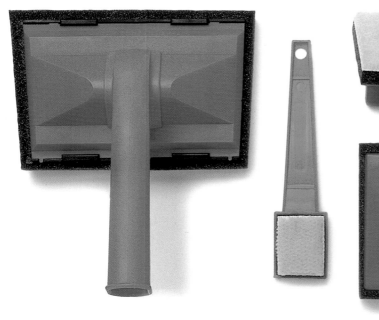

Paint pads
Pads come in a variety of sizes and shapes. Common sizes include a 4-inch pad for large flat surfaces, a 2-inch pad for large areas of trim, a 1/2-inch pad with tapered edge for narrow areas of trim. Some larger pads can be attached to extension poles.

Paint sprayers

The advantage of using a paint sprayer is that it can cover large areas quickly. There are two basic types. The paint sprayer most often sold at home centers and hardware stores is the airless model, which uses an electric pump to deliver the paint to the surface; the other type of paint sprayer uses compressed air to apply the paint. Newly marketed models of air sprayers—called HVLP sprayers—apply paint with less waste, or overspray. Until you are familiar with this tool, you will find spray painting the interior of a house tricky. Everything in the room that is not being painted must be covered, or overspray will lead to a long cleanup session. Also, it takes time to master the spray-painting technique of applying paint smoothly without drips or runs. Cleanup time is especially important with spray equipment, for if the sprayer is not thoroughly cleaned, it may malfunction or not work at all when you want to use it again.

Power spray equipment

Sprayers that use air atomize the paint during application, while airless models create a fine mist of paint. Some models are made for specific paint jobs, such as painting furniture or applying water-based paint to walls.

Solvents

As already mentioned, all paints contain some sort of solvent to keep the paint liquid. Solvents are also used to make the paint thinner when necessary and for cleanup (*p.126*). Some professionals like to use a little solvent on a new brush or roller to condition it before starting to paint.

You must always remember that, with the exception of water, all solvents are dangerous. They are flammable, irritating to the skin and respiratory passages, and poisonous. Solvents should be handled and disposed of with care. In many towns that means special handling by the town maintenance department (*p.128*).

SOLVENTS AND SAFETY

When cleaning painting tools with solvents, wear rubber gloves and eye protection. Not only are solvents flammable, but their fumes can cause a flare-up if exposed to an open flame. Be sure to extinguish flames and work only in a well-ventilated area. Also, make sure that you store solvents in sealed containers.

SOLVENTS AND THEIR USES

Type of solvent	Where to use it
Water	To clean brushes and rollers used with water-based paint. To remove dried drips and spills of water-based paint. To thin water-based paint.
Mineral spirits and turpentine	To clean brushes and rollers used with oil-based paint. To remove dried drips and spills of oil-based paint. To condition new painting equipment. To thin oil-based paint.
Denatured alcohol	To remove shellac. To recondition equipment used for water-based paint.

Other tools

There are a number of other tools you may find useful during your painting project. As with brushes and rollers, buy high-quality products to help ensure good results.

OTHER PAINTING TOOLS

1   **5-gallon roller bucket with roller screen**
2   **Small bucket**
3   **Paint-mixer drill attachment**
4   **Roller tray**
5   **Painter's mitt**
6   **Straightedge**
7   **Aerosol paint**
8   **Brush comb**
9   **Roller extension**

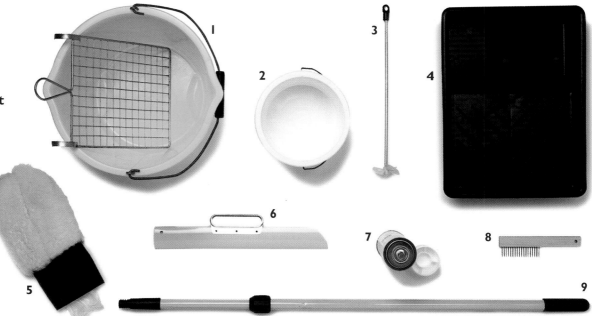

OTHER USEFUL TOOLS

1   **Painter's tape**
2   **Drywall knives**
3   **Putty knife**
4   **Scoring tool**
5   **Fiberglass joint tape**
6   **Wire brush**
7   **Utility knife**
8   **Drop cloth**
9   **Sanding block**
10 **Sandpaper**
11 **Rubber gloves**
12 **Sponge**
13 **Hook-bladed paint scraper**
14 **Flat-bladed paint scraper**

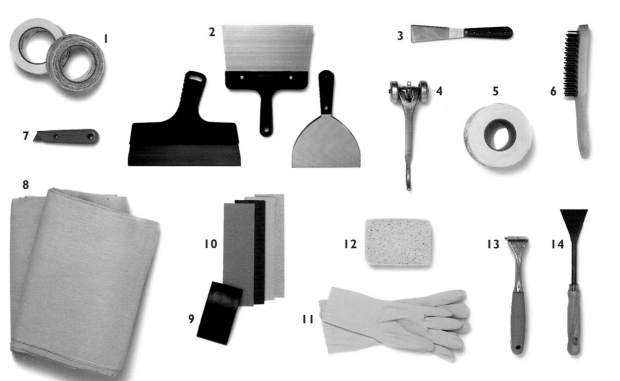

Ladders and scaffolding

Good-quality ladders and the right scaffolding allow you to paint the tops of walls and ceilings safely and efficiently. Even if you use a roller extension for reaching high areas, you will still need a ladder or work platform for cutting in (*p.130*) and for detail painting with a brush.

Ladders When shopping for a ladder, make sure it has the seal of the American National Standards Institute (ANSI). This certifies that the ladder meets manufacturing standards recognized by the industry. Ladders are available in three classifications, depending on how strong they are: Type 1, heavy duty, which is rated for loads up to 300 pounds; Type II, medium duty, rated for loads up to 250 pounds; and Type III, light duty, for loads up to 200 pounds. It is safest to always buy either a Type I or a Type II ladder.

Make sure that the ladder's hinges are strong and that the ladder is steady when it is open. Non-slip pads on the feet of the ladder will help to steady it. Also make sure that the steps of the ladder are wide enough to accommodate your feet comfortably. Wooden ladders should have a metal rod beneath each step for added support.

Choosing a good ladder
A quality stepladder should have a sturdy feel to it when you set it up in the store. Don't rely on your judgment alone however; look for a label that rates the load-bearing capacity of the ladder. Choose Type I or Type II for safety.

Scaffolding Ladders alone are insufficient for such jobs as painting stairwells and other high places. This is when you will need a work platform. A platform made of scaffolding saves you time because you don't have to continually climb up and down and move the scaffold, as you would if you used a stepladder. You can purchase a platform from a paint dealer or rent one from a tool-rental outlet. You can also make a platform from standard planking. If you use lumber, make sure that it is free of loose knots, checks, and splits. Use at least a 2-by-10-inch plank.

SETTING UP SCAFFOLDING

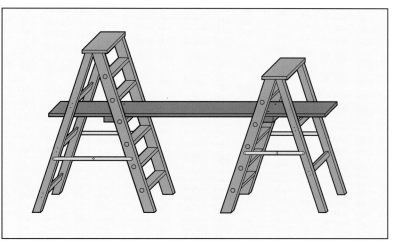

Create a work platform with two stepladders

Two stepladders can make excellent anchors for a scaffold. Be sure that the edges of the scaffold overlap the steps of the ladder by 12 inches. If the plank sags when you walk on it, move the ladders closer together.

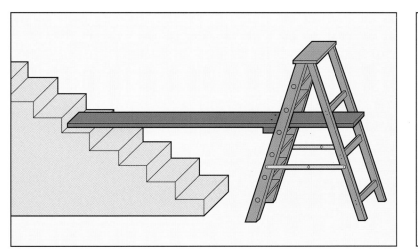

Create a work platform with a stepladder and stairs

Stairs can be used to anchor one end of a scaffold. The rise of the stair will help keep the plank in place. Add a cleat to keep the plank steady. If necessary, place an old towel on the stair to protect its finish.

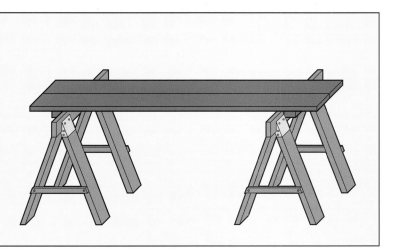

Create a work platform with two sawhorses

Two sawhorses can anchor scaffolding. Nail bracing between the legs at each end of the sawhorses to reinforce them. Add cleats to keep the scaffolding from shifting while you are working.

CHAPTER 3

PAINTING TECHNIQUES

Professional painters are good at what they do because they have expert techniques, refined by plenty of practice. This chapter provides the basics of painting techniques to help you achieve professional-looking results. It covers everything from preparing the paint and developing the best brush and roller techniques to tips on dealing with painting problems that you discover when the job is finished.

Working with paint

When you start a painting project, you will be using either a new can of paint or a previously opened can left over from another job. In either case, make sure that the components of the paint are properly blended and that the paint is free of lumps and foreign matter. Always ask your paint dealer to shake a new can of paint (a machine in the store does this). Even if you are not going to use the paint for a few days, this shaking will make your stirring easier when you are ready to begin work.

Use small containers You will find it easier to work from containers smaller than the gallon cans paint comes in. When painting with a roller, use a roller tray; when working with a brush, use a small paint bucket. Because both are lighter and easier to handle, they allow you to load a painting tool with paint more efficiently. A roller tray hooks onto the paint shelf of a ladder, and a small bucket isn't as cumbersome as a large can. In addition, both of these containers hold a small amount of paint that must be replenished as work progresses. This will remind you to stir the can so that its contents do not settle during the project. Transferring the paint to other containers keeps the lip of the can clean, making it easier to clean and close the can well at the end of the job.

Trays and buckets cost only a few dollars and are available in plastic or metal. The plastic models have the advantage of not rusting after you've cleaned them. If you are using trays and buckets you have on hand, be sure to wash and dry them thoroughly before adding paint. Since these tools are usually stored in basements and garages, they have a tendency to collect dust and dirt that, if not removed, could ruin a paint finish.

Thinning paint Although it is not necessary to thin paints for most jobs, some special applications, such as decorative finishes (*pp.75–77*), may require that the paint be thinned. Use water to thin water-based paint and mineral spirits to thin oil-based paint.

Experiment with different ratios of paint to thinner to find the one that works best. Work in small batches, carefully recording the ratios you are using. The only reliable way to test thinned paint is to apply it to the surface you want to cover and see if it produces the finish you want. If you are using scrap material as a test area, be sure it is primed and painted the same color as the area you want to cover. It is also helpful to view your results under the same lighting conditions as for the project. Once you have the proper proportions, you can mix a larger batch of paint.

PROFESSIONAL TIP

Before you begin to paint, be sure that you have enough paint on hand to complete the project. There is nothing worse than being forced to stop because you have run out of paint. Different batches of the same brand and color may vary. The problem will be greater if you are working with a custom color because the paint dealer may not be able to make an exact match of the paint that is already on the walls.

PREPARING THE PAINT

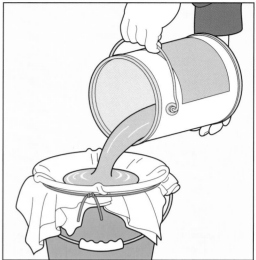

1 Opening the paint can
To pry open a can of paint, use a blunt, strong-edged tool. The edge of a 5-in-1 tool is made for this purpose. Pry up the lip of the can in several locations until you can lift the lid off. Don't be tempted to use a screwdriver, because you can damage the tool's head.

2 Stir to blend
Stir single cans of paint by hand with a wooden stirrer. Stir in a circular motion, occasionally scraping along the bottom of the can in a side-to-side pattern. Keep stirring until the paint has a smooth, uniform consistency and color. Consider using a power stirrer for large containers.

3 Avoid dirt or lumps in the paint
Before you begin working with a previously opened can of paint, make sure you filter out any dirt or other lumps. Use a double layer of cheesecloth or a paper or nylon screen. A large rubber band or string will keep the filter material stretched tightly over the lip of the bucket.

4 For thinning paint
Start with 8 ounces of paint and add solvent in 1-ounce portions. Don't add too much solvent at once; you can always add more but you cannot remove it. When testing a mixture, allow the paint to dry in order to judge the results accurately.

MIXING PAINT

When using more than one can of a custom-blended color, stir the paint by mixing, or "boxing," the cans. You will find that cans of custom colors may vary slightly from one to another, and boxing ensures an even color throughout.

Pour all the paint into a large container, such as a 5-gallon bucket. Mix the paint thoroughly and then pour it back into its original containers. If a large container is not available, add small amounts from each can to a clean paint bucket, stir, and return to the original cans. Stir each can and repeat the process until all of the paint has been thoroughly mixed.

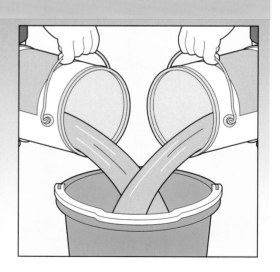

Brush technique

The type of brush you use will be determined by the type of paint that you are applying and the surface to be painted. As a general rule, oil-based paints go on better with natural-bristle brushes. Water-based paints should only be used with synthetic brushes because water damages natural hair (*pp.26–27*).

Applying the paint When painting walls and ceilings with a brush, apply the paint in small sections of about 2 to 3 square feet. The goal is to maintain a wet edge of paint as you work. This means that after you have applied the first brushload of paint, begin painting each succeeding load on an unpainted area and work back to the wet paint you applied previously. Never touch a freshly loaded brush to wet paint. This helps ensure that there will be no lap marks when the paint dries.

Painting a straight edge In most cases, painting a straight edge means following a guide that is already in place, such as the junction of a wall with a baseboard. If there are no guides available, use a plumb line for marking vertical lines or a carpenter's level for horizontal lines (*p.39*).

HOLDING AND LOADING BRUSHES

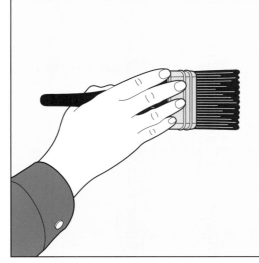

Gripping a narrow brush
Hold a narrow brush at the ferrule, between your thumb and forefinger, as if you were holding a pen. With a narrow-trim brush, shown above, that means curling your two smallest fingers up out of the way. You may need practice to do this comfortably.

Gripping a wide brush
You may find a large 3- or 4-inch brush more comfortable to use because you can place all of your fingers on the ferrule. There is no need to grip tightly. Keep your hand relaxed, maintaining just enough grip to guide the brush properly.

Loading the brush
Having transferred paint from the can to a small bucket, dip about 2 inches of bristle into the paint. Tap the brush against the sides of the bucket. Do not drag the bristles against the lip of the bucket, as this removes too much paint from the brush.

APPLYING PAINT WITH A BRUSH

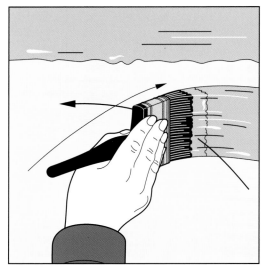

① Lay paint on

Apply the paint by laying it on with a few horizontal strokes: use one side of the brush and then the other side on the return stroke. Don't worry about filling in the empty spaces yet. Your goal here is to get the paint onto the surface.

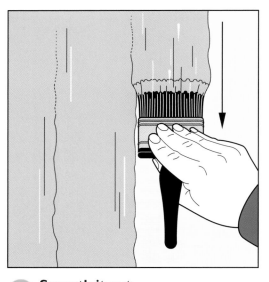

② Smooth it out

Without reloading the brush, use vertical strokes to spread the paint evenly over the surface. Brush away from the wet paint you applied previously and then work back. Flex the bristles of the brush slightly to get complete and even coverage.

③ Feather the edge

Tip off, or feather, the edges of your painted area: lightly brush as shown above but only with the very tips of the bristles, lifting the brush as you get to the edge of the painted area. This will blend the paint into a wet edge and create a new wet edge.

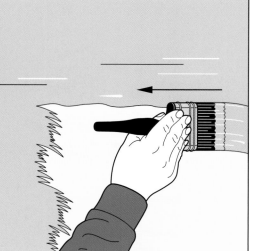

④ Keep a wet edge

Apply new paint to a dry area and work back toward previously applied paint. If you are painting woodwork, brush in the direction of the long dimension. Use the same feathering technique to blend and create a wet edge.

STAINING WOOD

Stain adds color to the wood while allowing the grain to show through. Staining is popular when a quality wood is used, such as in fine cabinetry, when the wood is clean-grained, without knots or checks. Most woodwork in homes, however, consists of lesser-quality wood and should be painted rather than stained.

Perfect your staining technique by practicing on scrap wood of the same material. Work in small sections and experiment with different densities. One technique involves applying stain liberally, allowing it to dry for a few minutes, and then wiping off with a clean cloth. Results will vary depending on the length of drying time and the amount removed with the cloth.

Some woods, such as pine and other softwoods, absorb stain unevenly even though they may be free of defects. Watch for this when testing. Try to compensate by wiping stain away quickly on porous areas and allowing it to set longer on less porous sections.

Brush with the grain

Although you should follow the directions on the can, stain is usually applied by following the grain of the wood with a brush. Apply with even strokes for a uniform finish.

HOW TO PAINT A VERTICAL STRAIGHT EDGE

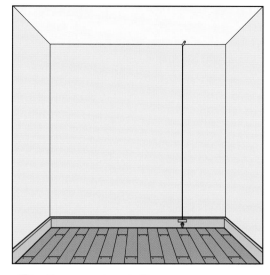

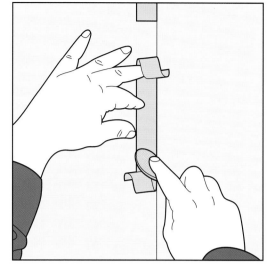

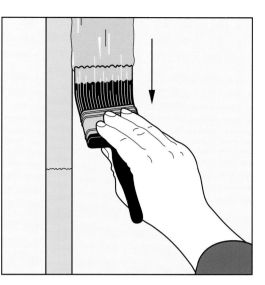

1 **Drop a plumb line**
For vertical lines, use a plumb bob and string. Insert a nail where the top of the line will be and attach the string to it. When the bob becomes still, the string forms a perfectly vertical line. Hold the line steady and tape it just above the bob.

2 **Tape in small sections**
Using the plumb line as a guide, apply painter's tape to the wall. Apply the tape in small sections because it is easier to maintain a straight line when working with small pieces of tape. Press it down to ensure that it bonds well to the surface.

3 **Paint the straight edge**
Use a 2-inch brush to actually paint the edge. Hold the brush on an angle, as shown, and slowly drag it down the wall about $1/8$ of an inch away from the line. Flex the bristles slightly and the paint will bead to the line.

HOW TO PAINT A HORIZONTAL STRAIGHT EDGE

1 **Leveling a horizontal line**
Use a carpenter's level to draw horizontal lines on the wall. Use a level that is at least as long as the line you wish to paint. The tool is perfectly level when the bubble is centered in the vial that is horizontal to the floor.

2 **Extending a horizontal line**
For lines longer than the length of the level, attach a string to one end of the wall and have a helper hold the other end. Use the level to adjust the position of the string. Alternatively, use a line level, a small level that hangs from the string.

PROFESSIONAL TIP

If you don't have a plumb bob, make one by tying a nail to both ends of a length of string. Fasten one end to the top of the wall and let the other hang free to get a plumb, or vertical, line. Don't use a chalk line for this or any other painting project. Once on the surface, the chalk is impossible to remove and will ruin the painted finish.

Roller technique

Using a roller on the walls and ceiling of a room will help you to finish the job more quickly than if you use a brush. The type of roller cover and the thickness of its nap (also called pile) will be determined by the type of paint you will be using and the surface you will be covering.

Using a roller You should be careful to load the roller with the correct amount of paint. Apply the paint quickly and evenly without leaving surface marks.

Power-roller technique The two keys to working with a power roller are learning to control the flow of paint and keeping the roller in motion while the paint is flowing. You should not allow the paint to flow the entire time, or you may create a mess as well as an uneven finish.

HOLDING AND LOADING A ROLLER

1 How to hold a roller
Start with an open palm and place the handle across the bottom of your index finger on a slight angle away from your fingers. Then close your palm. You can rest your thumb on the top of the handle or on the side.

2 How to load a roller
Dip the roller into the paint and roll it slightly to cover most of the roller. Now slowly roll the roller back and forth on the slope of the tray to distribute the paint evenly. Although the roller should contain a good deal of paint, it should not drip.

3 How to use a roller screen
Using the same technique as with a tray, fill the roller but avoid making any drips. Be careful not to dip the entire roller into the much deeper paint of the bucket or you may have a problem with paint running down the handle.

APPLYING PAINT WITH A ROLLER

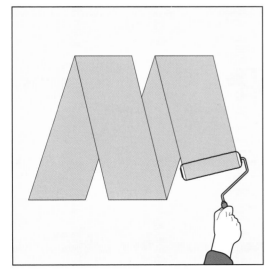

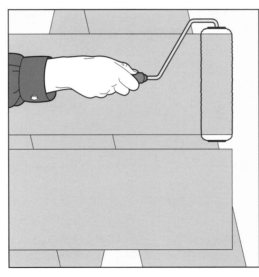

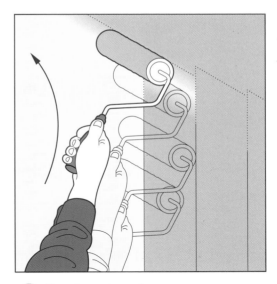

1 Apply paint
Apply paint in small sections about 3 feet square. Begin by laying on the paint in a zigzag motion, so that it looks like a large M on the wall.

2 Smooth the paint
Without reloading the roller, smooth the paint by making horizontal passes with the roller. Gradually work the new paint into the previously applied wet paint.

3 Feather the edge
Using vertical strokes, lightly feather the new paint into the old. Lightly roll the paint while lifting the roller slightly at the top and bottom of each painted area. This will blend the new paint with the wet edge and form a new wet edge.

USING A POWER ROLLER

Apply paint with a power roller
Always be sure to follow the manufacturer's directions, but in general let the paint flow to the roller head in brief spurts, avoiding a constant, heavy flow. Then use standard roller techniques to smooth the paint and blend it in with what is already there.

DEALING WITH PAINT BEADS

It is not unusual to find that roller lines, which are small beads of paint, form on the surface you are painting, especially if you have been painting for some time and the roller is saturated with paint. If they are not brushed out immediately, the roller lines may show up when the paint dries.

Beading occurs because you are applying pressure unevenly to the roller. This forces paint to the ends of the roller, where it forms drops. Avoid beading by applying less pressure to the roller. You can also try using an 18-inch roller. The larger size seems to minimize beading. Correct beads that are still wet by feathering the edge, as explained above.

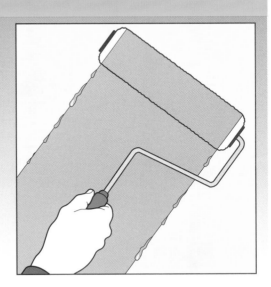

Power sprayers

A power sprayer will help you cover the walls of a room quickly. But the possibility of overspray means that you must cover doors, windows, and woodwork completely rather than simply applying painter's tape along the edges. It's also essential that you wear a respirator when using a sprayer. Because it takes so long to prepare a room properly, choosing to use a sprayer over rollers and brushes for interiors usually does not save any time.

Every spray gun will produce some overspray. You can reduce the amount of overspray by adjusting the tip of the gun to produce the correct spray pattern and by following the manufacturer's directions regarding air pressure and technique. Without cutting off the source of the room's ventilation, keep all windows and doors closed as much as possible to prevent breezes from carrying the paint to where it is not wanted.

Learn the pattern
Each tool has a different spray pattern, and it is important that you become familiar with the shape and size of the pattern before painting. Consult the directions for the proper distance to hold the spray gun from the work (usually 8 to 12 inches).

SPRAYER TECHNIQUE

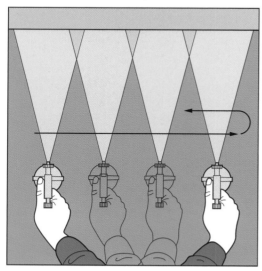

Spray from side to side
Spray in a side-to-side motion. As you move the gun to the right and left, bend your wrist and elbow to keep the gun tip perpendicular to the wall. Begin moving your arm before spraying and keep it moving after releasing the trigger to avoid paint buildup.

How to paint an outside corner
To paint an outside corner, stand directly in front of the corner and paint across it in short side-to-side strokes. Keep the tip of the gun moving perpendicular to the wall.

How to paint an inside corner
Face an inside corner and move the sprayer vertically from the top of the wall to the bottom. Make sure that you release the trigger at the end of the pass; this will avoid paint buildup near the bottom of the wall.

Paint pads

Paint pads are handy tools for painting woodwork and the edges of walls. The small, tapered pads are particularly useful for painting hard-to-reach sections of trim. If you are using an oil-based paint, make sure that you find out whether the pad is suitable for use with such paints, because some harsh solvents can ruin the pad. To paint with a pad, simply pull it along the surface to be painted. Some large pads have small wheels on the side of the painting surface that guide the pad along a raised edge, such as the trim around doors and windows.

However, it is difficult to get even results with pads when painting large open surfaces, such as walls and ceilings. Also, because the pads don't hold as much paint as brushes and rollers, and because they aren't able to cover surfaces so efficiently, they take more time to get the paint job done than other painting tools do. Although working the paint back and forth with a roller or a brush ensures even coverage, the same is not true of pads.

PAINT-PAD TECHNIQUE

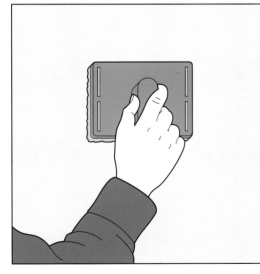

How to hold a large paint pad
Use a grip similar to the one you would use on a roller handle for large pads. Place the handle in your palm and close your thumb and forefinger around the handle. Your thumb should rest on the handle where it is most comfortable.

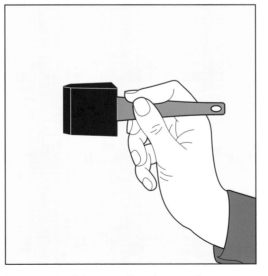

How to hold a small paint pad
When using a small paint pad for trim painting, grasp the handle between your thumb and forefinger. This provides the most control for detail work.

How to load a pad with paint
For large pads, dip the surface into a roller tray and remove excess paint by passing the pad over the raised areas of the tray. Dip smaller pads an inch or so into a paint bucket and remove excess paint by tapping the pad against the side.

Solving painting problems

Many paint jobs become problematic at some stage. Even the most experienced painter has to deal with mistakes. However, most problems can be either prevented or solved.

Some difficulties, such as blisters and specks in the paint, can be avoided by properly preparing the surface to be painted. Other flaws, such as brush marks, runs, and drips, are the result of poor application. Still others simply happen no matter how careful you are. The trick is to catch and correct minor problems before they become serious (the problems discussed below and on p.45 are all shown actual size).

PROBLEMS TO CORRECT BEFORE YOU BEGIN

Blisters Improper surface preparation causes paint to blister and peel. Painting walls and woodwork that are wet, dirty, or covered with numerous coats of old paint can result in a bubbling, peeling mess a short time after the fresh coat is applied. Avoid this problem by removing as much old paint and wallpaper as possible and then cleaning the walls thoroughly.

Specks Even a slight breeze can stir up small pieces of dirt and grit that will stick to freshly applied wet paint. Old paint that has not been strained can also contain dust and dirt that will end up on the surface you are painting. Protect your project by sweeping or vacuuming the room thoroughly before painting. Strain all previously opened paint (*p.36*).

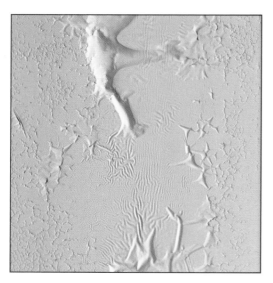

Fix leaks first
A wet spot on the wall prevents the paint from adhering properly and can cause a blistering surface. Sources of moisture, such as leaky roofs or plumbing problems, should be corrected before you paint.

Removing grit
Before the paint dries, remove the grit with the corner of a putty knife and brush out the mark. For dried dirt, sand clean and touch up with fresh paint, blending it in with the rest of the painted area.

SOME OTHER PROBLEMS

Here's how to deal with other problems that can occur during a painting project:

- It is not unusual for paint to change color slightly as it dries. If you think you were given the wrong color paint, allow a small portion to dry thoroughly and then determine whether it is the color you wanted.
- Light affects the color of paint. Avoid problems at the end of the job by viewing paint samples under all the lighting conditions, both natural and artificial, that will be encountered in the room *(p.15)*.

- Even professionals occasionally skip a spot when painting, especially when covering a large room. The only recourse is to go back and touch up as needed. Lap marks should not be a problem when using a flat or eggshell finish. If a glossy surface shows the touch-up lap marks, you may have to repaint the entire section of surface. In either case, it is always a good idea to keep a little extra paint on hand for touch-ups.

PROBLEMS TO AVOID DURING APPLICATION

Brush marks One way to avoid leaving behind brush marks is to apply paint in a thin, even coat. When painting woodwork, always paint in the direction of the grain. This will help to hide brush marks. Sometimes the brush is the problem. If you are using an old brush, test it first by painting a small area. Substitute a new brush if you are not getting the results you want.

Runs and drips Even the most careful professional painters must deal with drips and runs. Since drips aren't really a problem until they dry, check for them every 15 minutes or so. You should also inspect the last section of surface you completed after you have refilled your paint bucket or roller tray. If the paint is still wet, simply brush out the drip.

Sanding to hide brush marks
Sand new wood smooth to help hide brush marks on the completed project. Remove sanding dust with a tack cloth or a clean damp rag. Always paint in the direction of the wood.

Dealing with dry drips
Drips or runs that have become tacky should be allowed to dry. Sand out the imperfection and touch up with fresh paint. If the drip is still wet when you discover it, you can simply brush it out.

CHAPTER 4

PREPARATION

Preparing a room for painting starts with creating a safe and efficient workplace. That means removing everything you can from the rooms in which you will be working, including pictures, lights, and window treatments, and protecting furniture and surfaces that you don't want to be damaged by or splattered with paint. Spending some time and effort at this stage of the project will always be repaid with good results at the end.

Preparing the room

Empty rooms are easier to paint than rooms full of furniture. If you have the opportunity to paint a new house or apartment before moving in, by all means seize it. But in most cases you'll have to cover or clear furniture, pictures, and other objects before applying the paint.

The condition of the room to be painted will determine when to begin this phase of the project. As you will learn in the next chapter, all damage to walls, woodwork, and floors must be repaired before you paint. Repairing wallboard or plaster and sanding floors creates a lot of dust. Covering your furnishings before work begins will save time now and some cleaning bills later. If you are planning extensive repairs, you will want to give yourself time to do the work properly. This could mean moving and covering furniture a few days before actually painting.

Removing pictures and moving furniture will also let you see areas that are usually hidden, giving you some idea of the amount of repair work needed. If you are unsure of what has to be done before painting, make a preliminary inspection behind furniture a week or two before the project begins. Note what needs to be done on a legal pad. You may want to draw diagrams of the areas that need work. This list will come in handy when you go to buy repair materials and supplies.

This is also a good time to decide whether you want to employ a professional carpenter, drywaller, or handyman to do some of the more complicated repair work. If you use a professional, be sure to follow the steps outlined in this chapter before he arrives. A professional will also create dust and dirt; chances are he will not care about protecting your belongings as much as you do.

If the walls and the woodwork in the room are in good shape and require only minor repairs, you can wait until you are ready to begin painting before moving and covering the furniture. For an average-size room, start about an hour before painting.

The best way to start is by taking down pictures and other wall decorations and then work your way toward the center of the room. This includes books, china, and other display items even if the furniture that holds them will remain in the room. Remove anything that can be taken out of the room and store it in another area until the job is complete. The fewer objects left in the room, the better.

Whatever is left should be covered and placed away from the walls. Be sure to deal with any ceiling fixtures before you move furniture into the center of the room because you will need the space for your ladder to reach the fixture.

ROOM-PREPARATION CHECKLIST

- **Remove all blinds, shades, drapes, and curtains from windows.**
- **Roll up any carpets and cover them with drop cloths.**
- **Protect any exposed floors by covering them with drop cloths.**
- **Move all the furniture into the center of the room and cover it with drop cloths (*p.48*).**
- **Remove all pictures and any other wall hangings.**
- **Mask woodwork if necessary (*p.49*).**
- **Remove all switch plates and outlet plates (*p.50*).**
- **Switch off the electricity and remove any wall lights (*p.50*).**
- **Protect all the ceiling lights (*p.51*).**
- **Make sure that the complete work area is well lit (*p.51*).**
- **Make sure that the room is well ventilated (or wear a respirator if this is difficult—*p.52*).**

PROTECTING FURNITURE

Any furniture that will remain in the room should be placed in the center of the room and covered with either a plastic or a canvas drop cloth. Be sure you cover both the top and the sides of the furniture. Don't be tempted to use old sheets to cover furniture because paint can soak through the material.

On floors, use either canvas drop cloths or rosin paper (a heavy kraft paper available in large rolls). In either case, overlap the edges of the material and tape them. Avoid using plastic drop cloths on floors because they can be slippery.

The ideal arrangement protects your furniture while allowing you enough room to work comfortably. If you'll be painting the ceiling, you will need to reach it without stretching over pieces of furniture stacked in the middle of the room. Working with rollers equipped with extension poles will help you avoid this problem.

When working on walls, furniture should be far away enough from the perimeter of the room to give you space to work and move a stepladder easily. When moving furniture, remember that tall pieces can block the light you need when painting. To avoid this problem, first move the furniture and then position your work lights.

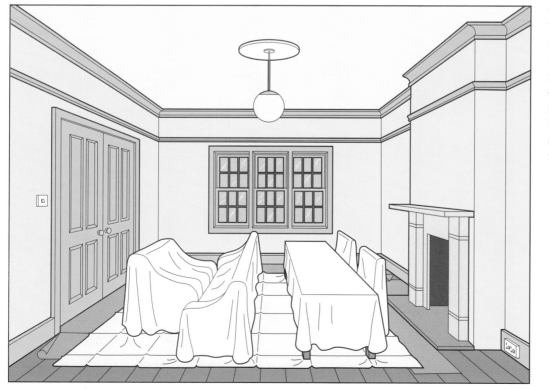

Getting the room ready

The goal here is to protect what you don't want painted while giving yourself a clear work area. Arranging furniture in a long, narrow configuration makes it easy to reach ceiling areas from either side of the furniture. Keep space clear under ceiling lights because you may have to paint around them with a brush and you will need to set up a ladder to reach the area.

Masking

Protect any surface that adjoins the one you will be painting with painter's tape. Be careful not to confuse it with the beige tape used for sealing packages. Painter's tape—usually colored blue or red—is specially designed for painting projects and will give you the best results. This tape can be applied and removed from a surface without its adhesives damaging the painted finish underneath. Although the tape should not harm the finish it is adhered to, try to make sure that you do not leave it on for too long—see the box to the right. Painter's tape is available in a variety of widths, ranging from ½ inch up to 12 inches.

Many people, especially professional painters, skip masking because it is time-consuming and adds to the cost of the project. However, if you are a novice painter, it is the best way to ensure a clean, crisp painted edge. Apply tape in small sections for easy handling. If you are painting the walls and ceiling of a room, mask the adjoining woodwork, including doors and window trim. If you are painting woodwork, mask the walls.

Choose a width of tape that is suitable for the surfaces that need protection. Generally, it is best to leave part of the tape edge farthest away from the paint loose for easy removal.

WHEN TO REMOVE PAINTER'S TAPE

Leave the painter's tape in place until the paint is dry to the touch. Removing the tape too soon can allow still-wet paint to run onto the surface you were trying to protect. Avoid leaving the tape on longer than is necessary because the tape's adhesive may stick to the surface and damage the finish it was covering.

USING PAINTER'S TAPE

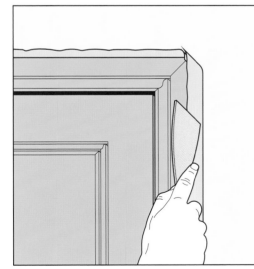

Applying the tape
Use a putty knife to smooth the painter's tape onto the surface being protected. Work with short pieces of tape to keep the edge as straight as possible *(p.39)*.

Masking woodwork
Smooth the edge of the tape closest to the paint against the surface but turn the outer edge up. This practice makes it easier to remove the tape when you have finished.

Masking windows
Use narrow painter's tape to protect glass. Apply the tape in small sections. It is helpful to use a blunt-edged tool to press the tape into corners.

Wall and ceiling fixtures

Before you start to paint, it's best to remove wall fixtures (be sure to turn off the electricity first), but leave ceiling fixtures in place. Wall fixtures are usually easy to reach and remove. Ceiling fixtures, such as chandeliers and ceiling fans, can be easy to remove but are usually heavy and cumbersome to reinstall. So it makes more sense to keep them in place and cover them.

Covering ceiling lights Use canvas or plastic drop cloths to cover ceiling fixtures. It is easier to form a protective bag with canvas, although you can achieve the same results with a very thin plastic. To protect the paddles on ceiling fans, use light-weight canvas or plastic.

Removing wall lights Remove wall fixtures so that you can paint as close to the rough opening as possible. This will give the paint job a neat, finished appearance. Turn off the electricity at the service panel and fuse box before removing the fixture (*p.54*). Protect the ends of bare wires by installing wire nuts or wrapping the ends in electrical tape. If you cannot remove a wall fixture, you will have to cover that as well.

WHAT TO REMOVE BEFORE PAINTING

Cover hanging ceiling fixtures.

Cover wall fixtures that can't be moved.

Remove wall fixtures.

Remove switch plates and outlet covers.

Cover thermostats.

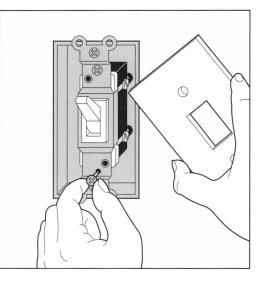

Removing a switch plate
Use a screwdriver to remove the screws and, if necessary, lever the switch plate away from the wall. Place the screws back in the holes in the switch box so that you won't lose them. Follow the same procedure when removing an outlet cover.

DEALING WITH WALL FIXTURES

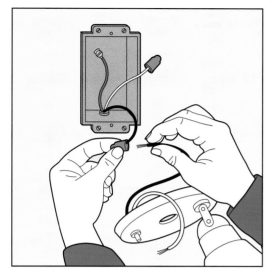

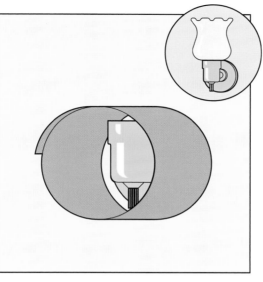

Removing a wall fixture
Undo the screws that hold the fixture in place, pull it away from the wall, and disconnect the wires. Then place wire nuts on the exposed wire ends in the box. Labeling the wires will ensure that you reconnect them correctly.

Covering a wall fixture
If the entire wall fixture can't be removed, just remove the shade. To protect the part of the fixture still attached to the wall, apply painter's tape around the edge and add a protective paper tube.

DEALING WITH CEILING FIXTURES

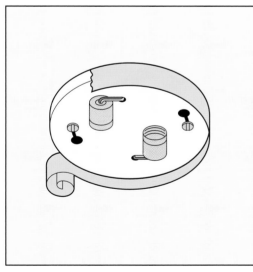

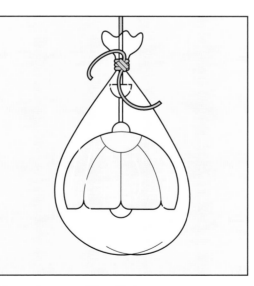

Removing a small ceiling fixture
For small ceiling fixtures, remove the outer glass globe. Unscrew the bulbs and apply painter's tape around the edge of the fixture. After you have painted around the light, replace the bulbs and use as a light source for the rest of the room.

Covering a ceiling fixture
Most ceiling fixtures have a collar or a trim rim to cover the rough opening in the ceiling. To protect the fixture, unscrew the collar and lower it slightly. Then wrap the rest of the fixture in plastic and secure it with a piece of string.

LIGHTING THE JOB
The room being painted needs as much light as possible. Proper lighting will help you to see immediately any patches that you have missed. It will also help you to spot any drips, beading paint, and other flaws while the paint is still wet and there's time to correct the problem. Since you will remove all window coverings and shades before you start, you will be using all of the available natural light. Add to the illumination by switching on all lights in the room and using portable work lights. If you have turned off all electric power to the room as a safety precaution, use portable lights plugged into outlets in other rooms.

Create as much indirect light as possible. For example, if you are painting the walls, make sure that you bounce the light off the ceiling, as this reduces glare and creates a uniform amount of light on the surface being painted. If you shine light directly onto the wall, you may create an area of shadow as you move about between the lamp and the wall.

Safety when painting

Interior house painting is one of the safest home-improvement projects that you can undertake. But there are still some potential hazards that must be avoided and a number of precautions to take to make sure the job goes smoothly and safely.

Start by reading the label on the can of paint you are going to use (*p.21*). The label not only tells you how to use the product safely but also provides you with first-aid advice. It is important to familiarize yourself with the procedures outlined on the can because they may differ from product to product. Other general safety rules to follow include:

- Keep all containers tightly closed when not in use.
- Keep paints and solvents away from heat and children.
- Keep a list of emergency phone numbers on hand.

PERSONAL PROTECTION EQUIPMENT

Although a painter's basic uniform includes long-sleeve shirts or sweatshirts, long pants, and gloves, you may require some other safety equipment. The most common pieces of personal protection equipment are:

Goggles These come in handy when you are painting overhead. They should also be worn when you are using chemical strippers or scraping loose paint.

Dust masks These should be worn when scraping away loose paint or sanding wood or paint.

Respirators These should be used when you can't ventilate a work area properly or if you are sensitive to fumes from paints and solvents. If you are using oil-based paints and solvents, make sure that the respirator is labeled "NIOSH/MSHA Approved for Organic Vapors."

Respirator

Dust mask   Goggles

LEAD IN PAINT

Until the 1970s, lead was a common ingredient of both interior and exterior paints. We now know that ingesting lead in old paint by either swallowing chips of it or breathing dust from sanding it can result in any one of a number of physical and mental problems, including malfunctioning of the kidneys, hyperactivity, and learning disabilities. Young children, pregnant women, and the elderly are most at risk.

The Consumer Product Safety Commission banned the use of lead in paint in 1978. This means that if your house was built or painted before 1978, it probably contains some lead paint.

Lead paint is a problem only if you sand it or if it is peeling or flaking from surfaces. Inside the house, lead paint is usually found on woodwork, doors, and windows. If there is a painted surface in your house in bad condition, have it tested for lead. Contact your local or state board of health for recommendations on where to find a licensed testing laboratory.

If your home has surfaces covered with lead paint that are in bad condition, then contact a lead-abatement contractor to remove the paint. The contractor will either remove the paint or encapsulate it. In either case, the contractor should be able to do the job without exposing you and your family to lead dust. Don't try to remove the paint yourself, because scraping loose paint will create dust that contains the lead.

It is also a good idea to make sure that young children are screened for the amount of lead in their bloodstreams. Most pediatricians recommend this simple blood test as a matter of course. The test is usually routine for all preschoolers.

FLAMMABLE MATERIALS

Some paints and solvents are labeled as flammable. The label will state "Warning: Flammable" or "Caution: Combustible Materials." With flammable materials, take these precautions:

- Open all doors and windows to increase ventilation.
- If you are working in a room with pilot lights, remember to extinguish them by turning off the gas. Do not relight pilot lights until the room is completely free of fumes.
- Don't smoke.
- Don't use electrical equipment that could create a spark.
- Clean up spills promptly and dispose of rags and other cleanup equipment safely. Ask your local waste-disposal authority how you should dispose of solvents.
- Close cans of flammable liquids when they are not in use.
- Keep a fire extinguisher handy.

VENTILATION

Some paints and solvents give off fumes that can lead to serious illness if you are exposed to them for long periods of time. Even short-term exposure can cause nausea and dizziness. You must also remember that some people are more sensitive than others to fumes, so that although you may not be bothered by them, they may make others ill. Reduce the possibility of exposure to fumes by following these rules:

- Open doors and windows for ventilation when painting and cleaning equipment.
- If you have difficulty breathing or if your eyes begin to water, leave the work area immediately. Go outside and breathe deeply. If the symptoms persist, call your doctor.
- If you can't ventilate the area properly, make sure you wear a respirator while working.

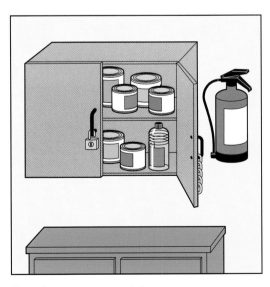

A paint-storage cabinet
Cans of opened paints and solvents should be stored out of the reach of children. The storage cabinet should have adequate ventilation and a lock on the door. If at all possible, mount the fire extinguisher near the cabinet.

54 PREPARATION

WORKING AROUND ELECTRICITY

When painting, you will have to remove switch plates, electrical-outlet plates, and, sometimes, entire light fixtures. Aside from the times you will be disconnecting wires when removing light fixtures, it is possible to complete the paint job without shutting off the electricity. However, if there are children or pets around, they may be tempted to touch the uncovered outlets. Since electrical outlets are usually located near the bottom of the wall, and therefore an easy target for young fingers, it makes sense to take the precaution of shutting down the electricity to the room in which you will be working.

Turn off the electricity at the junction box either by flipping the circuit breaker to the off position or by removing the fuse. Standard safety procedures when working near electricity include:

- If you take a break from painting, check to be sure the circuit is still off before resuming work.
- When shutting off the power, stand on dry planks or on a dry rubber mat. Never stand on a wet floor.
- When shutting off the power, keep one hand in your pocket to keep from touching metal with your free hand. Otherwise, your body could act as a conductor for the electric current.

TURNING OFF THE POWER

When removing wall or ceiling-light fixtures, be sure to turn off the flow of electricity to each fixture. You can do this by removing a fuse or turning off a circuit breaker in the electric service panel, which is located where the electric power enters your home.

To find the right circuit, turn on the lights and have a helper watch while you turn off each breaker. Check all the lights and outlets; sometimes more than one circuit serves a room. If you are in any doubt, be sure to consult an electrician.

SAFETY WITH ELECTRICITY

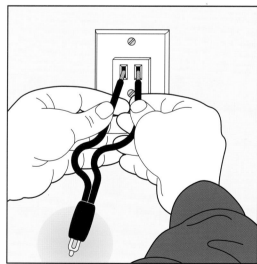

Test before touching
Don't assume that because one outlet in a room is off, other outlets in the room are also safe. Use a voltage tester to test each outlet. If any outlet is still live, go back to the service panel and find the switch or fuse that turns off the power.

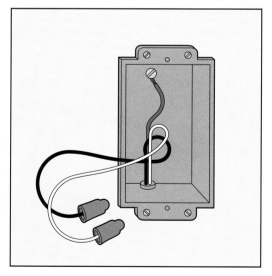

Cap exposed wires
When removing a ceiling or wall fixture, protect yourself and the wires that protrude from the ceiling or wall by capping them with wire nuts or electrical tape.

SAFETY WITH LADDERS AND SCAFFOLDING

Stepladders and scaffolding are among the most indispensable pieces of painting equipment (*pp.32–33*). Be sure to use them wisely. Protect yourself by always following basic safety rules:

- Never stand above the third step from the top on a ladder. It is easy to lose your balance when standing on the upper steps.
- Never put anything but a paint bucket or roller tray on the top shelf. The shelf is not designed to hold your weight.
- Don't be tempted to "walk" or jog the ladder along a wall while you are still standing on it. It is very easy to fall while trying to save the small amount of time it takes to climb down and carry the ladder to its next location.
- Don't attempt to repair a seriously defective ladder—avoid possible injury by buying a new one.
- Don't prop up a ladder on an uneven surface with an object such as a rock or a brick. You should create a stable platform by using wide boards.
- Don't set up a ladder in front of a closed, unlocked door.
- Don't place a metal ladder near electric wires.
- Make sure the braces on your stepladder are locked down.
- Choose straight planks without splits for scaffolding.

LADDER DO'S AND DON'TS

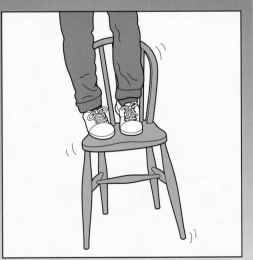

Brace planks and ladders
C-clamps can help hold planks steady when you use 2-by-10 lumber and two stepladders as a scaffold. In addition, the planks should overlap the steps by at least 12 inches.

Don't climb too high
Don't stand any higher on a ladder than the third step from the top. If you stand any higher, you will not have enough support to help you keep your balance. Also, the base of the ladder will be unstable, making it even more likely that you will fall.

Don't stand on chairs
Never use ordinary chairs to reach high spaces or as anchors for scaffolding. Kitchen and dining chairs are not designed to bear the weight of a standing person.

CEILINGS AND WALLS

The secret to achieving a good paint finish lies in how well you prepare the surfaces you plan to paint. You can get the best results from your labor—and the paint and equipment you have bought—by carefully cleaning and repairing the dents, cracks, and holes in the surface before you apply the paint. Attending to these details is just as important as the actual painting. Here's how to get perfect results.

First steps

Preparation is the essential ingredient of all good paint jobs. Ceilings and walls should be as clean and smooth as possible to provide a good base for the paint. There are a number of steps you may have to take to achieve this level of smoothness. It is important not to cut corners here.

Removing wallpaper Try to avoid painting over wallpaper. If you do paint over it, you are not likely to achieve the results you would get from taking the trouble to remove the wallpaper before painting. If you cannot remove it, make sure that all of the seams lie perfectly flat against the wall.

Preparing surfaces Allow yourself enough time to wash down the surfaces and make necessary repairs. Stand in the center of the room and check carefully for any damaged or greasy areas. Remove pictures and their hangers and pull furniture away from the walls to judge the condition of the areas that were hidden. Look for dents, cracks, peeling paint, and bumps in the finish. On walls and ceilings that have never been painted, look for nail holes that are not filled with joint compound and rough edges and seams that are not sanded smooth. All of these will interfere with achieving a perfect finish.

Using the correct tools and materials Clean the ceilings and the walls with any type of household cleanser that will remove the grease and dirt. Professional painters frequently use trisodium phosphate (TSP), a strong, water-soluble concentrated cleanser that leaves no soapy residue. You can apply and rinse off all cleansers with ordinary sponges.

While you are washing the surfaces, you will have a good opportunity to examine them closely. The next few pages show you how to remove wallpaper and repair most kinds of damage you will find. You can use spackle or joint compound for filling small holes and cracks in drywall or plaster walls. But the materials used for large repairs will depend on what the wall is made of. Plaster walls will require plaster patches. Holes in drywall can be filled with new drywall and sealed with drywall tape and joint compound. Apply these materials with putty knives and drywall knives. These knives have flat blades and are available in a variety of widths. Use fine-grit sandpaper for smoothing out both plaster and drywall repairs.

In addition to the specialist painting tools listed on this page, you will also need tools found in any home tool kit, such as hammers, screwdrivers, saws, and pliers.

MATERIALS AND TOOLS

Cleaning materials
Sponges
Drop cloths
Spackle
Joint compound
Plaster patches
Drywall tape
Putty, drywall, broad-blade, and utility knives
Sandpaper, sanding block or sponge
Home tool kit
Wallpaper remover
Wallpaper steamer
Scrapers
Steel wool
Seam roller
Primer
Wire lath
Drywall, drywall saw, tape, and screws
Brushes, rollers, and roller extensions
Painter's tape
Ladders
Paint
Paint solvent

Removing wallpaper

The type of wallpaper used, how it was applied, and what the wall underneath it is made of will determine how best to remove the paper. Strippable vinyl wall coverings that were pasted on properly prepared walls are the easiest to remove. Simply insert the corner of a putty or drywall knife under a raised seam and work a section of the paper loose. Then peel the paper from the wall.

Using liquid removers You may find that your wallpaper doesn't peel off easily, or that it was installed over another layer or several layers of wallpaper. In either case, use warm water or a liquid wallpaper remover to dissolve the adhesive, then peel off the paper. If the paper still won't come away, consider renting a wallpaper steamer for removal.

Using steamers Wallpaper steamers can be rented from tool-rental companies and some paint stores. Since rental tools rarely have complete written instructions, you may need to ask the dealer to explain how to use the tool. Two people can develop an efficient routine when using a steamer: while one person scrapes the paper, the other can be applying steam to the next section.

REMOVING WALLPAPER WITH LIQUID

1 Score the paper
Use a razor scraper or a utility knife to cut through the wall covering without damaging the underlying wall. These cuts will allow the liquid to seep through to dissolve the wallpaper paste.

2 Apply the liquid
Apply the water or wallpaper remover with the help of a spray bottle or a garden sprayer. Work in small areas. If the solution dries before you can remove the paper, you will have to wet the area again.

3 Remove the paper
Use a broad-blade knife to scrape away the paper. Keep the blade of the knife flat so that the corners do not nick the surface of the wall. Clean off any paste residue with warm water or fine steel wool.

REMOVING WALLPAPER WITH A STEAMER

Loosen and remove paper

Hold the steam plate against the wall until the paper is loose. Remove the paper with a broad, flat-blade knife. Clean up any paste residue with warm water.

FIXING LOOSE SEAMS

If you have to paint over wallpaper, make sure that the paper is free of bubbles and that all seams lie flat. Fix loose seams by prying the edge up with a pointed object and dabbing paste on the wall. Press the paper into the paste and roll it with a seam roller. Then apply an oil-based primer.

REMOVING MILDEW AND WATER STAINS

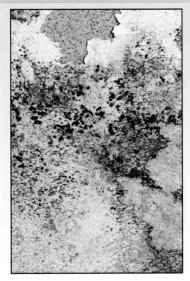

Removing mildew

Mold and mildew grow in damp, unventilated areas. Most of the time, it occurs in kitchens and bathrooms, especially in the grout of ceramic tiles, but it can also be found on woodwork and the surface of walls and ceilings. Remove mildew with a solution of 1 cup of chlorine bleach to about 1 quart of water. Wet the area with the solution (wear rubber gloves when working with bleach) and allow it to soak for a few minutes. Scrub with a soft-bristle brush and then rinse. Allow to dry before painting.

Removing water stains

A water stain on a ceiling or wall means there is a leak somewhere. Often, the problem can be traced to loose flashing around a skylight or chimney. Before painting, find the source of the leak and have it repaired. If the area around the stain is crumbly and soft, replace it with new material (*pp.60–67*). If the surface is simply stained but still in good condition, cover the stain with a primer that contains shellac. If you don't, the stain will eventually show through the new paint job.

Repairing plaster

Walls and ceilings usually develop small cracks and chips over time. These must be repaired because no matter how small the damaged area may be, it will always show through a new coat of paint.

Filling nail holes The nail holes you find in the walls after removing pictures, shelves, and other wall hangings must be filled before you start painting.

Sealing cracks in plaster To fix a small crack, you will need drywall-joint compound or spackling compound and sandpaper. Check the labels of the products you buy for drying times and material compatibility.

Replacing plaster Drywall-joint compound can be used to patch holes in plaster that are less than three inches across. Larger areas should be treated with a plaster patch.

In most cases, minor repairs take only a few minutes to complete. However, the material you use to make the repair will need time to dry before you cover it with paint.

FILLING NAIL HOLES

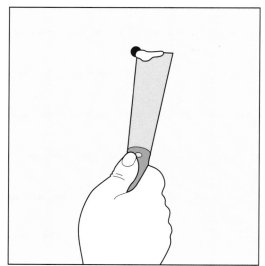

1 Force compound into the hole
Use the edge of a narrow putty knife to force drywall compound into the hole. You can also push compound into the hole with your finger.

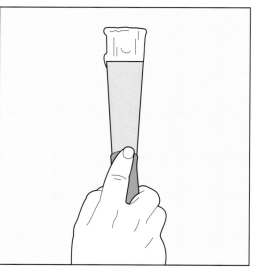

2 Smooth out with a putty knife
Since nail holes are small, it is easy to level off the patch with the surrounding walls with just a putty knife. Finish by dabbing on some primer.

PAINTABLE PAPERS

Sometimes a sound wall may have so many small flaws that repairing it seems overwhelming. You can cover such walls with paintable wallpapers or wall liners. These liners are white, heavy-duty papers that are applied with wallpaper paste. They are available where paints are sold. To paste, butt seams against each other—do not overlap—and smooth out wrinkles and bubbles with a wallpaper brush. Once on the wall, the wall liners can be painted with water-based paints. Wall liners cannot be used to cover large holes or splits in the wall.

SEALING CRACKS IN PLASTER

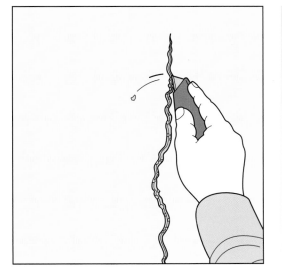

1 Clean out the crack
Use a sharp utility knife to clean out loose debris. You can also use the pointed end of a bottle opener. While wearing goggles, blow into the crack to remove any very fine dust.

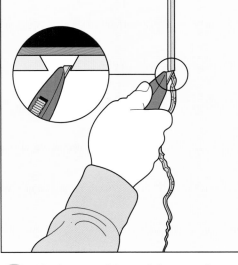

2 Undercut sides of the crack
To undercut the sides of the crack, angle the blade of the knife to scrape out a thin bottom layer of undamaged material. The goal is to give the patching compound something fixed to adhere to.

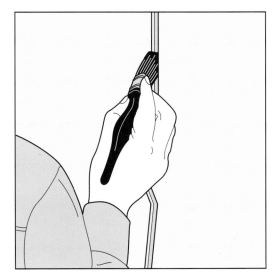

3 Dampen with a small brush
Dampen the undercut crack and the surrounding area with a small brush that has been dipped in water. Be sure to use the water sparingly, because the surface should be damp, not wet.

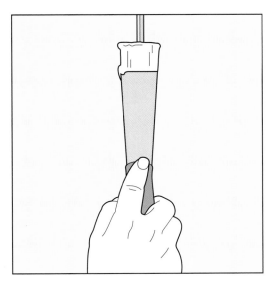

4 Fill the crack
Apply the joint compound with a putty knife. Force the material into the crack. Make one stroke down the length of the crack to remove excess compound.

5 Sand to smooth
Allow time for the joint compound to dry thoroughly. Sand with a sanding block until the repair blends with the surrounding wall. Apply primer.

PROFESSIONAL TIP

You can use sandpaper, a damp sponge (see p.67), or a sanding screen to smooth joint compound. If you need to sand a large area consider using a sanding screen. The screen is an abrasive surface that does not clog as it sands; it is clipped to a handled tool.

REPLACING PLASTER

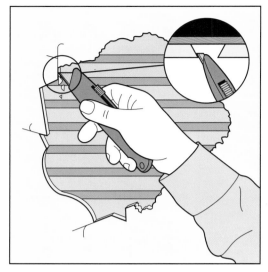

1 Undercut the edges of the hole
On lath-and-plaster walls, clean and undercut the edges of the damaged area and the surface of the old lath.

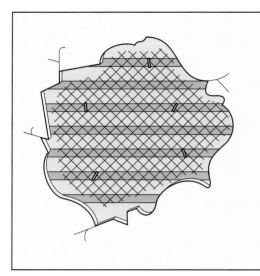

2 Staple lath in place
Attach a piece of wire lath over the wood lath, using drywall screws or staples, as shown here.

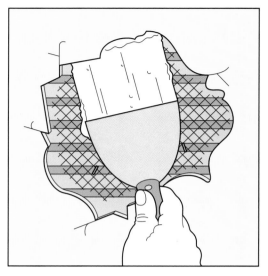

3 Create a patch
Mix up some patching plaster according to the package directions and apply a ¼-inch-thick coat to the hole. Be sure to work the patch into the undercut edge of the damaged area.

4 Score patch with a putty knife
Score the patch with the edge of a putty knife and allow to dry. Doing this provides a base for the next layer of plaster by giving it something to adhere to.

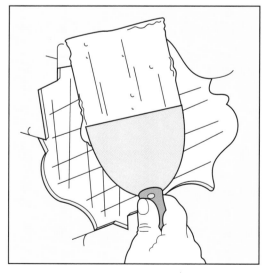

5 Apply a second coat
Dampen the first coat of plaster and apply a second coat. The plaster should now be about even with the surrounding wall. Allow to dry.

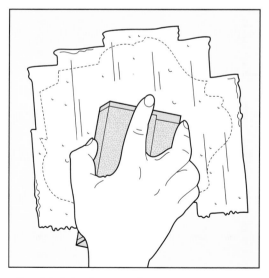

6 Finish the patch
Apply a finish layer of joint compound to the patch. When it is dry, use a sanding block or a sanding sponge to feather the edges of the compound into the surrounding wall and create a smooth finish. Apply primer.

Repairing drywall

Drywall, or wallboard, has largely replaced plaster in both new construction and remodeling projects. Drywall is not only easier to install than plaster, but it can be repaired with plugs made from the same material. You will find it useful to keep a few extra small pieces handy for repairs. There are many different types of drywall on the market. For patching purposes, be sure to buy the thickness that matches the material that is already in place. Doing so will ensure that patches lie flush with the existing wall. Following are some of the problems that may occur in drywall, and their solutions:

Dents This material is easy to damage, and it is not unusual for even the most minor of accidental bumps to result in a small dent. Check for depressions where the backs of chairs press against walls. Dents can be filled with a joint compound.

Popped nails The nails used to secure wallboard to the studs in the wall can sometimes work themselves loose. You will see either a protruding nail or a small bump where the nail is pushing up the joint tape and previous coats of paint. Either drive the nail back in or remove it before repairing.

Large areas of damaged drywall If there is a large amount of damage to the drywall, you must add cleats to support the replaced section. Cut the drywall with a drywall saw or a utility knife. To trim a large sheet of drywall, use a straightedge and a utility knife to score the paper facing. Lift the panel and snap it along the scored line to break the gypsum core of the panel. Use the utility knife to trim away the paper backing.

Small holes Any hole that measures less than 5 inches wide can be fixed with a patch attached by means of a paper flange rather than a cleat.

Damaged corners Outside corners made of drywall are easily damaged. They can be repaired by rebuilding the corner with joint compound.

Loose drywall tape Sometimes the wall is in fine shape but the tape between drywall sheets is peeling away. You should repair this by removing the loose tape and retaping.

HOW TO TAPE A DRYWALL JOINT

Drywall seams are concealed with a combination of drywall tape and drywall-joint compound. The tape keeps the compound from cracking when dry. You should follow this sequence for taping a joint:

- Smooth fiberglass mesh tape over the seam.

- Apply a thin, even layer of joint compound with a 5-inch drywall knife to cover the drywall tape. Allow to dry.

- Use an 8-inch knife to apply a second coat over the first, feathering the edges. Allow to dry.

- Use a 10-inch knife to apply the third coat, feathering the edges. Allow to dry.

- Sand rough spots between coats.

- Smooth final coat with a damp sponge (p.61).

REPAIRING A DENT IN DRYWALL

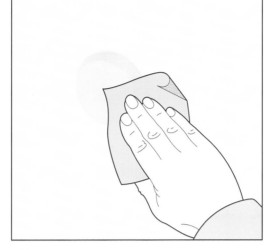

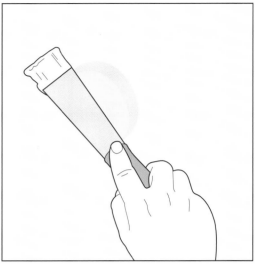

1 Roughen the surface
Sand the dent lightly with fine-grit sandpaper. This will give the patching material something to grip.

2 Apply compound
Apply joint compound with a putty knife. For deep dents, apply it in thin layers, waiting for each layer to dry before applying the next. When it's dry, sand with fine sandpaper on a sanding block and prime.

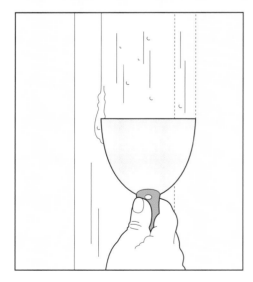

Feather the edges
To feather the edges of the second and third coats of drywall compound, press harder on the outside edges of the knife. You may have to make two strokes to completely cover the previous coat.

REPAIRING A POPPED NAIL IN DRYWALL

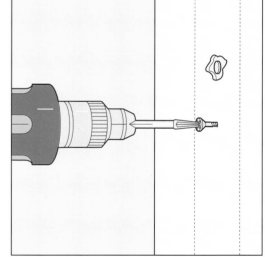

1 Drive in the old nail
Scrape away the paint and other material to expose the head of the nail. Drive the nail back into the wall and use a nail set to tap it below the surface. Remove a nail only if you can do so without damaging the wall surface.

2 Drive in a drywall screw
Drive a new drywall screw (they have more holding power than nails) 1 or 2 inches below the loose nail. Set the screw just below the surface of the wall without damaging the face of the wallboard. Cover the repair with joint compound and prime.

REPLACING DAMAGED DRYWALL

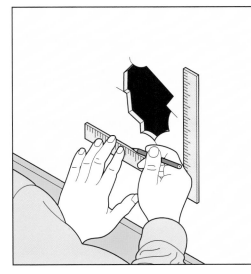

1 **Create straight edges**
Since most damaged areas have irregular shapes, use a straightedge to trim the surrounding wallboard to create a square or a rectangle. Doing so will make it easy to create a tight-fitting patch.

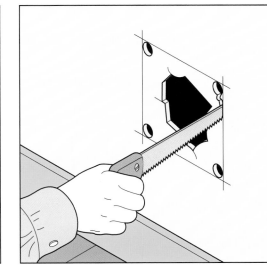

2 **Cut a hole out of the drywall**
Carefully drill starter holes in the corner of the marked box. Use a drywall saw, as shown, or a sharp utility knife to cut along the marked lines. Be careful not to apply too much force and crack the drywall further.

3 **Add support**
Use 1-by-4-inch cleats to support the damaged area. Fix the cleats with drywall screws, as shown. Part of each cleat should be hidden by the wall; the other part should be exposed in the opening.

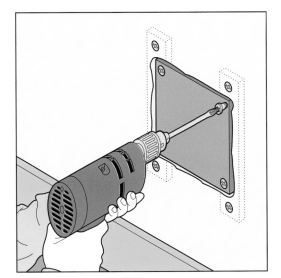

4 **Cut and fill**
Center the patch in the hole. Attach the new drywall with screws, driving the screws slightly below the surface.

5 **Apply tape**
Apply joint tape to the seams. Then apply joint compound with a drywall knife, smooth out, and sand.

FOR WIDER DAMAGE

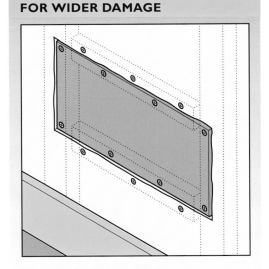

Use studs for support
If the damaged area is extensive, cut the drywall back to the center of the adjacent studs and use them for support. Screw cleats to the top and bottom edges of the hole.

SMALLER HOLES IN DRYWALL

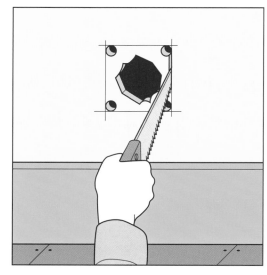

1 **Trim the edges**
Trim the edges of the damaged drywall area until you have created a square or a rectangle around it. Then measure the size of the new opening.

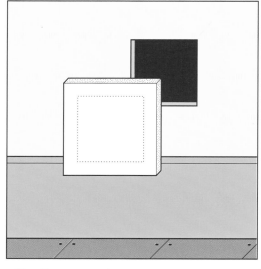

2 **Cut a patch**
Cut a patch of drywall that is about 1 inch larger than the hole on all sides. Place the drywall on a table, with the white side (which will show on the wall) facing down.

3 **Draw the dimensions of the hole**
Draw the dimensions of the hole on the patch of drywall. Center the outline so that there is an equal amount of excess material on all sides.

4 **Snap the sheet**
Working on one side at a time, score the lines so that you can snap the sheet to break the gypsum core. If you have trouble snapping it along the score lines, use the edge of a table to break the core.

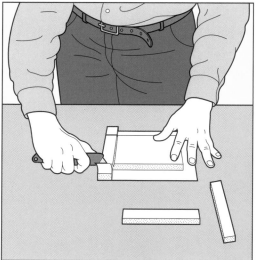

5 **Scrape away the backing**
Scrape away the backing and the core, but leave the paper facing in place. This will create a small flange that will overlap the edges of the hole. Apply joint compound around the edges of the hole.

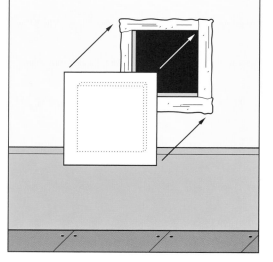

6 **Fit the patch**
Fit the patch into the hole and press the flange into the joint compound. Allow this to dry, and then apply another coat of compound. Sand the patch smooth and prime as needed.

REPAIRING A DAMAGED CORNER

1 Patch the corner
Use a large trowel or a piece of lumber as a form for the drywall compound. Apply compound until the damaged area is filled. Then slide the form out of position.

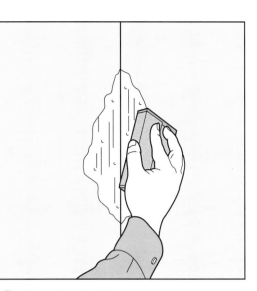

2 Sand to finish
Wait for the compound to dry thoroughly (it usually takes 24 hours), and then sand with a fine sandpaper until the patch is even with the surrounding wall.

REPAIRING LOOSE DRYWALL TAPE

1 Cut away any damaged tape
Pull and cut away any loose tape from the wall. Remove all of the tape until you reach a section that still fully adheres to the wall. Sand the edges of any remaining tape.

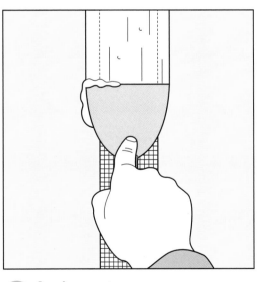

2 Apply new tape
Apply fiberglass mesh tape to the drywall seam. Cover this with a thin layer of joint compound. Allow to dry and apply further coats *(p.64)*.

Final preparation of walls

You should not find any popped nails on a new wall-board wall, but you will see dozens of small depressions left by nails and screws. Those that are located along the seams of two sheets of drywall will be covered by drywall tape and joint compound. You should fill the others with drywall-joint compound and then smooth with a knife.

Construction, especially drywalling, raises a lot of dust, which can make a terrible mess of the painted finish. It is important, therefore, to clean the walls and ceiling with a dust mop before painting new drywall or plaster. Then sweep up all dust and dirt from the floor. Finally, vacuum all horizontal surfaces, including windowsills, fireplace mantels, and moldings.

Now is a good time to make a final check of the room to make sure that all drywall joints are smooth and that they are even with the surface of the wall. If you find that any joint compound has hardened on the floor or on a part of the wall where it should not be, scrape and sand it off.

Prime bare plaster or wallboard *(p.24)*. After clearing away all preparation materials, you are ready to paint.

PREPARING UNPAINTED SURFACES

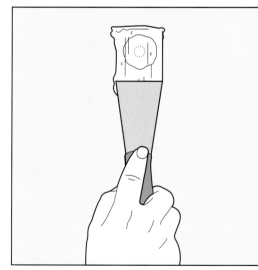

① Apply joint compound
Use a putty knife to apply joint compound to the small dimple left by a drywall nail or screw.

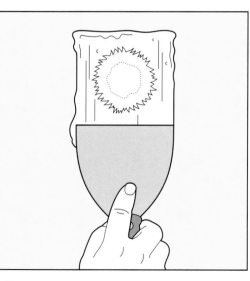

② Apply more coats
Allow the first coat to dry and follow with a second and a third coat. Sand rough spots and smooth with a damp sponge.

PEELING PAINT

Paint usually peels from walls and ceilings because the surface was not prepared properly the last time it was painted, a leak has loosened the existing paint, the wrong type of paint was used originally, or the wall was damaged in some way. Whatever the cause, you must remove the loose paint before redecorating to give the new coat a good surface to adhere to.

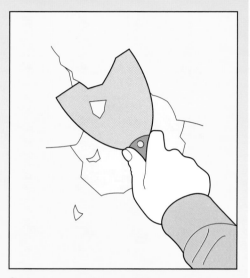

Scrape away loose paint
Use a flat-blade paint scraper to remove loose paint from ceilings and walls. Work away at the paint until you come to a section that cannot be removed with the scraper. Using a medium-grit sandpaper, sand the edges of the paint left around the scraped area. The idea is to create a smooth, seamless transition between the existing paint and the bare wall. Switch to a fine-grit paper for a final smoothing. Prime the bare spot.

Painting ceilings and walls

Once you have prepared the ceiling and walls, protected what needs to be kept safe from splattered paint, and have all of your equipment and tools at hand, it is time to get started.

Getting ready Begin by setting up a staging or work center, an area in the room where you can mix paint, refill roller trays, and keep equipment you are not using at the moment but may need to use later. An out-of-the-way corner equipped with a sturdy table covered with a drop cloth will work fine. Store paint that you do not need immediately under the table, along with any extra brushes, roller covers, and rags.

PAINTING CEILINGS

When painting an entire room, always work on the ceiling first. The advantage of this is that any paint splatters on walls and woodwork can be cleaned up easily or painted over later.

Start at the narrow end of the room and work across the width of the ceiling to help avoid lap marks. If you are painting the walls of the room later, save time by allowing an inch or so of the paint to overlap onto the wall when cutting in *(p.130)*. You will find it easier to paint a straight edge on the wall than on the ceiling. If you are not painting the wall, use a brush to cut in at the corner where the ceiling and the wall meet. Some rooms have crown or ceiling moldings at the top of the wall. These serve as useful guides when you are painting and make it easy to cut in.

If two painters are working at the same time, start at opposite ends of the narrow part of the room and work toward each other. This means that your wet paint edge will be advancing toward your partner's. Don't be tempted to have one person cut in while the other rolls. Not only could the person using the brush get ahead of the painter using the roller, but the border could dry before the rest of the ceiling is painted, producing lap marks.

Wear a cap and goggles when painting ceilings. Using roller extensions will help the work move along quickly because you won't have to continually climb up and down the ladder when moving to a new section. Be sure that any ceiling fixtures are protected by plastic drop cloths.

Lighting ceilings When painting the ceiling, start near a window and work back. In other words, paint in the same direction as the light. Because the natural light source will be in front of you as you work, you can see and correct mistakes as they happen. This method also helps to hide roller lines.

PROFESSIONAL TIP

Practice using an extension
Before loading the roller, practice handling the extension. Start by holding the handle with your hands 18 inches apart and then experiment with different grips until you are comfortable.

HOW TO PAINT A CEILING

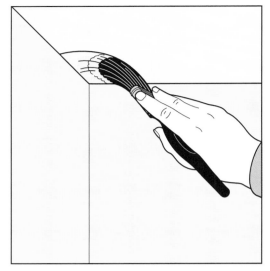

1 **Cut in with a small brush**
Begin in the corner and use a 2-inch brush to paint the border between the wall and the ceiling. Flex the brush's bristles to draw a straight line along the edge. Paint an area that is about 6 inches wide. Accuracy is more important than speed at this point.

2 **Paint the corners**
Go back to the corner and pull the paint out along the other side of the angle with the brush. This will help to prevent paint buildup in the corner that might eventually drip down the wall.

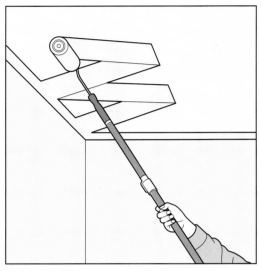

3 **Use the roller**
Work on small sections of the ceiling at a time. Dip the roller in the paint reservoir and roll along the sloped surface of the roller tray. The roller cover should be saturated but not dripping with paint. Apply the paint in a zigzag pattern, so that you form a large M or W.

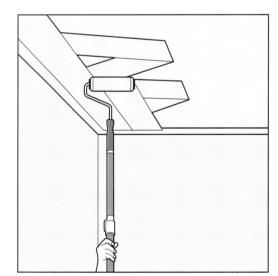
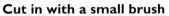

4 **Smooth out the paint**
Without reloading the roller, make strokes lengthways across the zigzag pattern. The goal here is to smooth out the paint over the entire section.

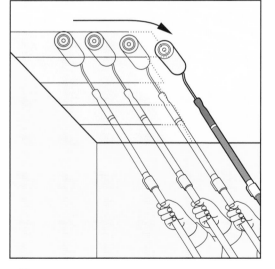

5 **Feather the edge**
Rolling toward the unpainted areas, feather the edges of the painted area by lifting the roller slightly near the edge of the section. Then begin another section, working across the narrowest part of the room.

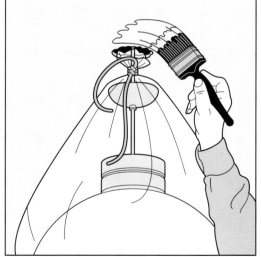

6 **Paint around ceiling fixtures**
Use the trim brush to paint around a ceiling fixture. Once you have enough room to maneuver the roller comfortably, continue to use it for the rest of the area.

PAINTING WALLS

When you paint a room, the walls account for most of the surface area you will cover. In fact, painting the walls of even a medium-size room is a big job. Fortunately, though, there are only a few basic techniques that you need to master in order to achieve results worthy of a professional.

You can roll paint on a wall, or you can brush it or spray it on. If you choose rolling—as most people do—you will still have to brush the paint on around the edges. If the wall is made of unpainted wallboard or plaster, apply a primer first.

Preparing to paint By now, you will have painted the ceiling and prepared the walls. You will also have masked the edges of doors and windows and removed or masked all switch plates, outlet plates, and light fixtures.

Taking cues from the room Remember that the shape and layout of the room will often tell you where to start painting. Start on the wall with the most open wall space. Save the wall that requires the most cutting in around windows and doors for last. However, if you are making a late start, paint the smallest wall first. That way, when you stop for the day, you will still have been able to finish painting an entire wall.

Where to begin Right-handed painters usually start by painting the upper-right-hand corner and left-handers, the upper-left-hand corner. This ensures that your body and your free hand will always be in front of an area of unpainted wall. If you should happen to lean against or touch the wall, you will not be touching wet paint.

Painting high walls The easiest way to paint a high wall is with a roller extension (p.69). Remember to use a sturdy stepladder to reach the top of the wall—never stand on a chair or stool.

PROFESSIONAL TIPS

- Give your walls a fresh coat of paint to improve the look of your entire house prior to selling it. Most real estate agents recommend choosing a neutral color, such as white or beige, to improve your chances of making a quick sale.
- If you are planning on finishing up tomorrow what you can't get done today, don't bother to clean your roller. Store it in a plastic bag overnight (p.127). Before resuming painting, make a few practice passes on scrap material to "recondition" the roller cover.
- The techniques on the following pages will help novice painters to achieve total coverage on their walls. However, some professionals use a roller extension to paint walls because handling the extension is easier on the shoulders than using the short handle of a roller, especially when painting is their full-time job. After you've mastered the basic techniques, consider using the extension on the walls to avoid fatigue.

HOW TO PAINT A WALL

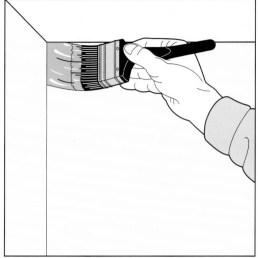

1 Cut in with a small brush
Using a 2-inch brush, apply paint where the ceiling and the wall meet to create a wet edge that measures approximately 3 feet across and 6 inches down.

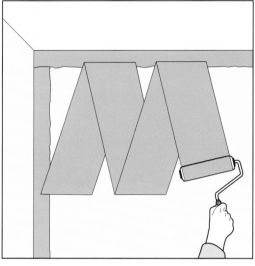

2 Brush below the juncture
Keep the bristles of the brush just below the juncture of the wall and the ceiling and, using long, even strokes, apply light pressure to bend the tips of the bristles slightly. This will force the paint to bead and fill the gap between the top of the brush and the ceiling.

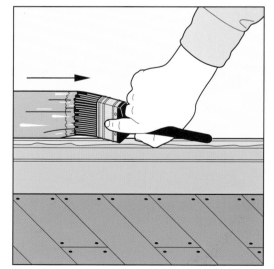

3 Apply the paint with a roller
Without waiting for this strip to dry, use a roller to paint the open areas of the wall beneath. About 3 feet below the wet edge, lay on the paint in a vertical zigzag pattern that looks like a big M. This section should measure about 3 by 3 feet.

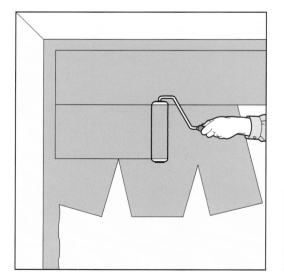

4 Even out the paint
Without loading the roller with more paint, smooth out the paint using horizontal strokes. Make sure that the entire section is covered with fresh paint and that the new paint blends with the wet edge. Work quickly, but don't rush.

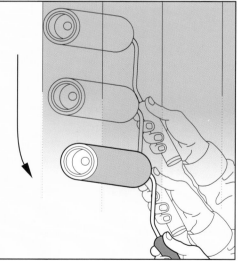

5 Feather the edges
Use the feathering technique *(p.41)* along still unpainted portions of the wall so that they will blend in easily with fresh paint. Then, begin again with the roller, making sure you blend in the new paint with the wet paint of adjacent blocks.

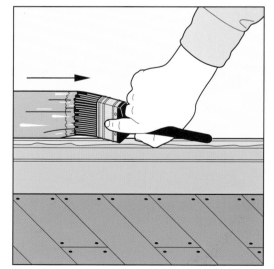

6 Paint along the baseboard
At the bottom of the wall, where you will have too little room to use the roller, use the 2-inch brush to paint a border just above the baseboard.

7 Paint around windows or doors
When you come to a window or a door opening, use the brush to paint a border along the edge of the frame's woodwork closest to the wall area you are painting.

8 Fill in with a roller
Fill in the open area of the wall with the roller. Then, again with the brush, paint the border along the top of the opening and at the juncture of the ceiling and the wall. Fill in this open area with the roller. Repeat the process below a window.

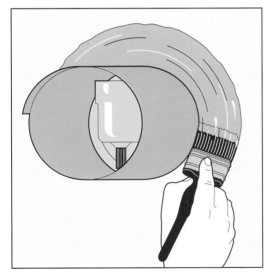

9 Paint around light fixtures
If you haven't already shut off the electric service panel, do so now, and disconnect and label the wires (p.50-51) or mask light fixtures. Apply paint around the opening with a narrow brush.

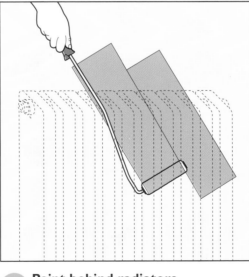

10 Paint behind radiators
Apply paint with a radiator brush. If you can't find a radiator brush, use a mini-roller instead.

OTHER CHOICES

Painting walls with a brush
Many people feel they get better results using a brush rather than a roller on walls. While it is true that brushes are easier to direct and are less likely to splatter, the job will take longer to complete (pp.26–27).

Power rollers and power sprays
Although ordinary rollers and brushes are the preferred tool for applying paint to walls, power rollers and power sprays will cover large walls more quickly (pp.29-30).

Remember to wear goggles, as well as a face mask or a respirator, when using a power spray.

PACING YOURSELF
The best time to take a break is after you have completed an entire wall. If this isn't possible, stop at a window or a doorway. Never stop painting for any length of time in mid wall. If you stop, the demarcation line between the two areas will show plainly when the job is finished.

Textured finishes

Textured paints contain additives that cause the paint to dry to a rough finish much like that of stucco. For the purpose of aesthetics, these types of paints add a certain depth or texture to what would ordinarily be a smooth surface. For more practical purposes, they can be used to hide the cracks and other imperfections that develop in walls and ceilings. Use ordinary household tools, as well as painting tools, to create unusual patterns in the textured surface. Experiment with sponges, crumpled pieces of newspaper, and mason's trowels. Ready-mixed textured paints are the easiest to use, although these paints are also available in powdered form.

REPAINTING TEXTURED FINISHES

If you are repainting a textured finish, use a long-nap roller but keep a brush handy. If the texture is very pronounced, the paint may begin to drip as you apply it. If this happens, smooth the paint with a brush immediately after rolling.

TEXTURED FINISHES

Adding texture with a brush
Roll the paint on the ceiling or wall, as shown here, and then use an old paintbrush to add texture. Dab the ceiling with the bristles, or slap the flat edge of the bristles against the ceiling.

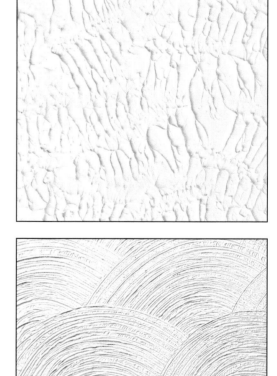

Using a whisk broom
Roll the paint on the ceiling or wall. Hold the bristles of a whisk broom at an angle of about 60 degrees to the surface. Make one continuous sweep to form a half-circle pattern and lift the bristles from the surface. Repeat the process, overlapping about half of the preceding half circle.

Decorative finishes

Most of this book deals with painting the inside of your home with solid colors of paint. But you can create unusual effects by mixing ordinary paints with transparent glazes. A top coat of glaze allows parts of a solid base coat to show through, which creates the illusion of depth and an interesting merging of colors and shades. Both oil- and water-based glazes are available. If you are using water-based paint, select a water-based glaze.

The three techniques shown here are only a few of a number of decorative finishes. Some mimic the look of natural materials, such as marble and wood, while others create unusual effects. No matter which ones you try, be sure to practice on scrap material first so that you can judge how a finish will turn out.

DRAGGING

This method works best on doors and woodwork rather than on large expanses of wall. Prepare the surface for painting and apply an eggshell base coat with a brush. Mix the glaze and the paint. Experiment with a glaze that is darker than the base coat. Keep the dragging brush clean between strokes.

THE METHOD FOR DRAGGING

Drag in straight lines
Apply the glaze. While the glaze is still wet, drag a dry dragging brush over the surface. Keep the lines as straight as possible. Once you start dragging a section, don't stop until you reach the edge. Overlap the rows of lines slightly.

The finished effect of dragging
Protect the surface with two coats of clear urethane varnish.

MATERIALS AND TOOLS FOR DRAGGING

Paints
Glazes
Brushes
Varnishes

SPONGING

Prepare the walls or woodwork as you normally would for painting, including priming. Decide on a color scheme that includes a base coat, which will be the foundation of the treatment, and one or two other colors. These other colors can be lighter shades of the base coat, or they can contrast with it. Use an eggshell- or satin-finish paint for the base coat. When you mix the glaze into the sponging paint, add a little at a time until you achieve the shade you want. Test the effect on scrap material.

Begin in an inconspicuous corner of the room until you gain confidence in your technique. Work slowly, and make sure you do not over-sponge. This will make the impressions too dense and will result in an overall muddled appearance. Wait for the first sponge coat to dry before applying the second color.

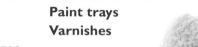

MATERIALS AND TOOLS FOR SPONGING

Paints	**Paint trays**
Glazes	**Varnishes**
Natural sponges	

SPONGING OFF

Take a little paint off
For a slightly softer look, try dabbing a surface with paint. Then, with a sponge dipped in solvent (mineral spirits if using oil-based paint, water if using water-based) and squeezed until just damp, dab lightly over the still wet paint.

THE METHOD FOR SPONGING

1 Sponge on the first color
Wear rubber gloves to dip a section of the sponge into the paint-and-glaze mixture. Squeeze it out and press the sponge on newspaper to remove excess paint.

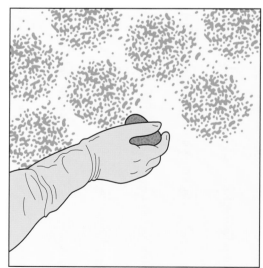

2 Dab on the surface
Begin dabbing on the surface to be painted. Leave small spaces between the dabs. Vary the position of your wrist and sponge as you work.

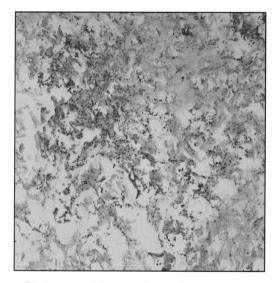

3 The finished effect of sponging
One coat of sponging will create the effect shown here. You can add a second coat in another color once the first is dry. Finish with two coats of urethane varnish.

RAGGING

Prepare the surface as you would for painting and apply an eggshell base coat. Then create a glaze by mixing the glazing material with paint. Interesting effects can be obtained by using a darker or lighter version of the base coat for the glaze coat. While one person rolls on the glaze, a second follows behind to do the ragging. The idea is to use the rag to lift off part of the glaze.

For the rag, use any lint-free material. Cotton rags are the traditional material used for ragging, although you can also use burlap, canvas, or even crumpled newspaper to form a pattern. If using fabric, stay away from synthetic materials, as they do not absorb paint as readily as natural fibers do. Whatever you use, have plenty on hand. As you work, the rags will become saturated and they have to be replaced frequently.

MATERIALS AND TOOLS FOR RAGGING

Paints   Solvent
Glazes   Varnishes
Lint-free rags

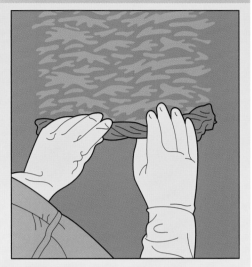

RAG ROLLING

Roll the rag up and down
Rather than holding the rag in the palm of your hand, try rolling it up like a cylinder, then rolling it up and down the surface. Overlap the rows slightly. This will keep a wet edge and avoid lap marks. Change rags often to maintain the pattern.

THE METHOD FOR RAGGING

1 Dab the surface with a rag
Dampen a rag with solvent, crumple it up, add paint, and dab at the surface. Vary the position of your hand to make interesting patterns. Develop a rhythm with your partner. Clean or change the rag when it becomes saturated with paint.

2 The finished effect of ragging
Protect the finish with two coats of clear urethane varnish if desired.

The finished effect of rag rolling
Rag rolling produces a consistent pattern over a large area. To maintain the pattern, use only one type of material. If you are using old clothing, remove seams, buttons, etc.

CHAPTER 6

WOODWORK, DOORS, AND WINDOWS

Painting a room's woodwork and the trim around doors and windows opens up a number of design possibilities. You can choose a bold color to contrast with the color of walls and ceilings, or use the woodwork as a frame to highlight the color of the walls. If the woodwork is the most distinctive feature in the room, this is your opportunity to enhance its beauty. If the woodwork is quite ordinary, you can make it blend into the background.

Paints for woodwork

While many types of wood used in furniture making are so beautiful that their grain and natural color are left exposed, much of the woodwork found in homes relies on painted finishes for its beauty. This is especially true of most houses built within the past 40 years. However, older homes and even some newer houses in certain parts of the country have stained woodwork. If you are adding new moldings or doors to this type of house, you will want to stain the new wood to match what is already there.

Making repairs Moldings and casings around windows and doors hide seams and rough openings in plaster and wallboard, creating a finished appearance. They also protect walls from bumps and dirty hands. For this reason, high-sheen paints are usually chosen for these surfaces. In fact, woodwork may be the last bastion of oil-based paints in homes. Of course, there are a number of very good reasons for selecting water-based paints, including ease of cleanup. Review the differences between these two types of paint *(p.22)* before making a selection.

Painting technique Painting the woodwork of a room requires a slightly different technique than covering the walls and ceilings does. The sweeping motions of using a roller give way to the control and precision of using a brush on a small surface. Also, brush marks are more likely to occur on wood than on plaster or drywall.

THE ORDER FOR PAINTING WOODWORK

When painting woodwork, start at the top of the room and work down: ceiling moldings, doors, windows, chair-rail moldings, then baseboards. Save wear and tear on your knees when painting baseboards by wearing knee pads or by kneeling on a cushion.

The edges of woodwork are sometimes curved or very narrow—less than one inch—making it difficult to paint them neatly. Vertical edges of windows and door casings not only are narrow but also are often at an angle that is difficult to reach easily with a paintbrush. It is sometimes a good idea to paint the woodwork before painting the walls, overlapping the walls slightly as you work on the woodwork. You'll find it easier to paint a straight edge along a wall than along the edges of narrow or curved woodwork. Be sure to protect freshly painted woodwork when working with a roller on walls.

Preparing woodwork

Whether it has been painted before or not, wood must be properly prepared before being painted. In general, this means filling any cracks and holes and then sanding the surface. Even previously painted surfaces must be sanded, especially if they were painted with a glossy sheen. The sanding gives the surface "tooth," or something to which the new paint can adhere. This is very important if the original paint is oil-based and you plan on covering it with a water-based paint. As an alternative to sanding, you could apply a chemical deglosser. Deglossers are liquids that help the new paint bond to the old one.

Be sure surfaces are clean. Remove fingerprints and stains with a household cleanser and allow to dry. Clean oily woodwork with trisodium phosphate according to label directions.

Just as you surveyed your walls and ceilings to judge the extent of necessary repairs, do the same with the woodwork. Pay special attention to the woodwork around doorways and baseboards near furniture, as these areas are subject to a lot of abuse.

Making repairs Fill holes or nicks in woodwork with wood filler. Some professional painters use glazing compound to fill small holes. Designed to hold glass in window frames, this putty-like substance does not shrink and is easy to apply, hence its popularity among professionals. Latex caulk can be used to fill seams that open up between two pieces of molding.

Removing peeling paint Peeling or loose paint can ruin a new paint job. Protect your paint job by carefully scraping away loose material and sanding the edges to provide a smooth transition between the sanded area and sound paint. In some cases, you will have to strip away the old paint in order to provide a good surface for the new paint.

Preparing windows and doors The wood on windows and doors should be free of defects and dirt and grease, as should any other wood surface. Before painting, remove all hardware, such as locksets and doorknobs.

MATERIALS AND TOOLS

For preparatory work
Sandpaper
Chemical deglosser
Cleaning solutions
Wood filler or
 glazing compound
Caulk and caulking gun
Electric palm sander
Vacuum cleaner or rags
Putty knives
Paint scraper
Primer
Heat gun (optional)
Power sander (optional)
Paint stripper (optional)
Wire wool

For painting
Paints and stains
Brushes and rollers
Masking tape or heavy paper
Screwdriver
Hammer and nail set
Utility knife
Sawhorses

MAKE THE SANDING SHEET FIT THE SURFACE

Manipulate abrasive paper so that it is easy for you to use. For example, to sand concave surfaces, wrap the paper around a section of hose or pipe. Large flat surfaces can be sanded with a sheet of paper wrapped around a wood block.

PREPARING PAINTED WOOD

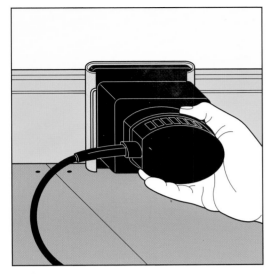

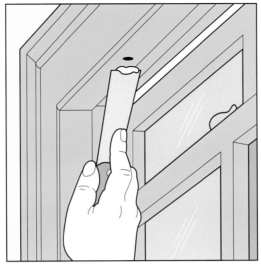

1 **Roughen the surface**
Prepare glossy sheens to receive the new paint by sanding with 150-grit sandpaper. On wide sections of molding or casings, use an electric palm sander. Wipe the surface with a cloth or vacuum it. Then repair and fill any holes and nicks.

2 **Fill any holes**
Use a putty knife to apply wood filler or glazing compound. Smooth with the knife so that the repair is even with the surface of the wood. If the first layer of filler shrinks, apply a second layer. Allow the repair to dry, then apply primer.

HIDING WOOD KNOTS

3 **Deal with any loose paint**
Scrape away loose paint with a paint scraper. To avoid gouging the underlying wood surface, hold the blade nearly parallel to the surface. Remove as much old paint as you can. Stop when you reach an area of fully adhered paint.

4 **Sand the edges**
Finish the repair by sanding the edges of the old paint. This will help to create a smooth transition between the new paint and the old. Prime the repair.

If wood knots are showing through the old paint finish, begin your project by spot priming with a shellac-based primer (*p.24*). If you skip priming, the knots will eventually bleed through.

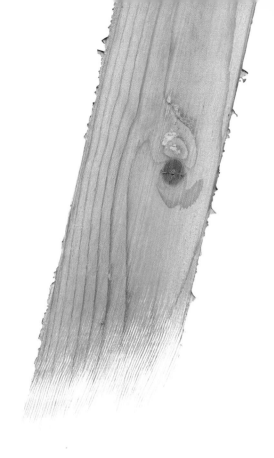

STRIPPING WOODWORK

It is usually unnecessary to strip the woodwork in a room unless you are planning to remove layers of old paint to reveal antique moldings or millwork. If the old paint is still in good condition, proceed as shown on pages 80–81. But if the old paint finish is flaking, peeling, or blistering, correct the problem by stripping the paint from the damaged section.

There are three ways to remove paint: using a heat gun, sanding the surface, or applying chemical paint removers. All three methods have their pluses and minuses. Heat guns make the work go quickly but if not used properly can scorch the woodwork or cause a fire. A power sander is useful for removing paint on large sections of flat woodwork. Sanding provides a smooth finish but produces a lot of dust. Chemical strippers are available as liquids, pastes, and gels. Although they provide quick results, they are caustic, and some produce noxious fumes. If you do use a chemical stripper, choose pastes or gels for vertical surfaces.

When stripping or sanding, try to close the rooms off from the rest of the house by hanging sheets of polyethylene plastic over doorways. This keeps fumes (be sure the room is well ventilated) and sanding dust from getting into passages or other rooms.

USING A HEAT GUN

Strip paint with a heat gun
Heat guns cause the paint to bubble and blister. As the paint bubbles, remove it with a flat-blade knife. Keep the heat moving in front of the knife. Direct the heat gun away from the wood surface as you scrape the paint from the knife into a metal container.

USING A POWER SANDER

Strip paint with a power sander
First, use a coarse-grit paper in the sander. Always keep the sander moving to avoid damaging the wood surface. Sand in the direction of the grain. When all the paint is removed, smooth the wood surface by hand-sanding with a fine-grit paper.

USING CHEMICAL STRIPPERS

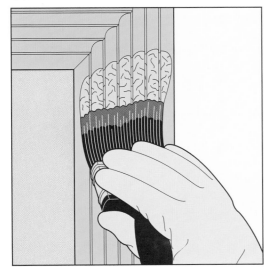

1 Apply the stripper with a brush
Wearing protective gloves, apply the chemical stripper with a brush and then wait for the time specified in the directions on the product's label. Let the stripper do the work of dissolving the paint.

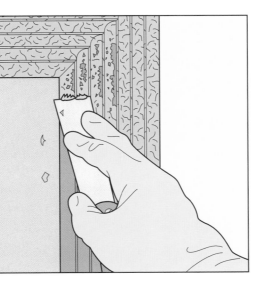

2 Remove the paint with a knife
Remove the loose paint with a flat-blade knife, disposing of the waste in a metal container. Work carefully to avoid damaging the wood. Apply a second coat of stripper if necessary.

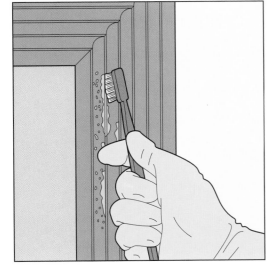

3 Remove the paint from grooves and crevices
Use an old toothbrush to remove paint from grooves and crevices. Don't try to remove the paint from creases with a wire brush, as it will scratch the wood.

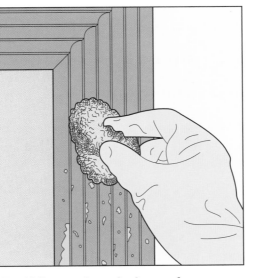

4 Wipe and wash the surface
You may have to wipe the surface down with more stripper and steel wool before wiping it with water to remove all traces of the stripper. Follow the directions on the product's label. Sand the surface lightly before priming.

USING PAINT STRIPPER

If you are worried about nicking woodwork with a steel blade when you are removing the paint with a stripper, try using a plastic stripping knife. You can also use special stripping pads made of synthetic material. These pads will not damage wood, they will not rust if you are using a water-based stripper, and they last longer than steel wool.

SAFETY TIPS
- Wear safety glasses for all stripping methods.
- Wear protective gloves when scraping away paint removed with a heat gun.
- Keep a fire extinguisher handy when working with a heat gun.
- Wear a dust mask when sanding.
- When using chemical strippers, keep the area well ventilated and wear a respirator. Never smoke or allow others to smoke while you are working with chemical strippers.
- Wear rubber gloves and a long-sleeve shirt when using chemical strippers.
- Keep children and pets away from all stripping tools and materials.
- Dispose of stripped paint properly (p.128).

PREPARING BARE WOOD

As with any surface about to be painted, bare wood must be clean, dry, and smooth. Clean with a household cleanser if necessary. For stubborn grease marks and oil-based spots, rub with a rag dampened with denatured alcohol (wear rubber gloves).

Carefully check all the moldings and casings. Spot sand rough edges and fill nail holes, cracks, and dents (p.81). Make sure that all nails are punched below the surface of the wood.

After sanding, make sure that you remove all sanding dust before it becomes trapped under a coat of primer by wiping the woodwork with a damp cloth or vacuuming thoroughly. Professional furniture refinishers use a tack cloth specially treated to remove dust. If you are painting only a window or two or a short section of new molding, invest in a tack cloth. For larger jobs, use a damp—not wet—rag or sponge to remove dust.

Filling joints The joints where two pieces of door or window casing meet at a corner sometimes separate. Caulking materials are used as fillers for open joints. There are many different types of caulk on the market. For filling cracks in wood, choose either plain latex or acrylic latex, as both of these are compatible with wood and can be painted.

Filling openings
Fill a separated joint in a window casing with caulk. Apply it with a caulking gun. This will seal out both air and water. After you have filled the opening, wipe the surface smooth and prime.

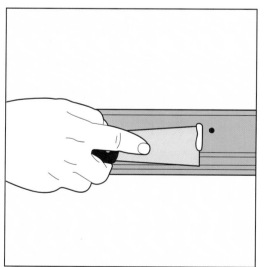

Filling nail holes
Fill nail holes in new moldings and casings with wood filler or glazing compound. Push in a small bit with the edge of a putty knife or your finger. You can use the same technique for small nicks and dents in the wood. Sand if necessary.

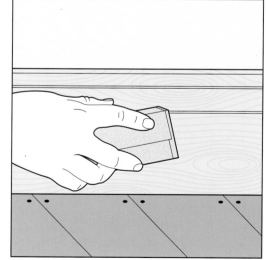

Smoothing rough spots
Use a fine-grit sandpaper to smooth the rough spots. Before priming, wipe the surfaces with a tack cloth or a damp rag. Allow to dry and then prime.

Sanding difficult areas of wood
Smooth narrow areas, such as muntins, by cutting the sandpaper into strips and grasping the muntin between your thumb and forefinger. Sand in an up-and-down motion (or from side to side on horizontal muntins). Wipe with a cloth before priming.

Priming and painting woodwork

The right tools Although the walls and ceilings of a room may make up a larger area, you need just as much precision when painting the woodwork of an average-size room. For moldings and casings, you'll be using 2-inch brushes and spending a lot of time painting straight edges along walls and ceilings. Rather than masking these areas, use a straightedge to mask as you go.

Priming the surface Apply a coat of primer to all bare wood before painting. The primer will seal the surface of the wood, preventing the paint from soaking in, and will provide a good base for the finish coats.

If a water-based primer has slightly raised the grain of the wood, sand with a fine-grit sandpaper and remove sanding dust with a damp rag before applying finish coats. Oil-based primers can also be used, even if you plan on applying a water-based paint as a finish coat. However, oil-based primers usually cannot be painted for 24 hours after they are applied *(see p.24)*. Mask any adjoining surfaces that will not be painted.

When to prime moldings Some professionals like to prime moldings before they are installed. Stand the section of molding on end or place it on a work surface covered with newspaper and then paint. Since there is no need to paint a straight edge, the primer will go on quickly. However, spot priming of repairs, such as filled nail holes, is still required.

Check the drying time Be sure to check the label on the primer can to see when you can apply the finish coats. Although the primer must have time to dry completely, it is important to apply top coats as soon as possible after drying. Primers left uncovered for too long become poor paint surfaces.

Painting woodwork When the primer is dry, sand lightly and wipe away the dust. Rough up the surface of painted wood with a fine-grit sandpaper or a liquid deglosser before painting.

Painting moldings Work from a stepladder or scaffolding. Start wherever you are most comfortable, but remember that right-handed painters will find it easier to work from left to right.

Painting built-ins Bookcases, cabinets, and other built-ins should receive the same preparation as other woodwork. Use a washable-sheen paint on these areas. If possible, remove shelves before painting; otherwise, follow the sequence on page 87.

PRIMING WOOD

Apply in the direction of the grain
Brush on primer with a 2-inch-wide brush in the direction of the wood grain. Don't be concerned if it appears to be splotchy and uneven. The finishing coats of paint will smooth out the surface.

AVOIDING MASKING

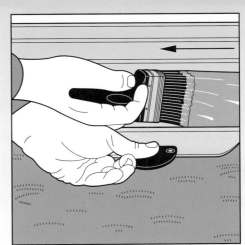

Masking *(p.49)* takes a great deal of time. To avoid masking, hold a straightedge in your free hand to protect surfaces as you paint. To paint the baseboard, hold the straightedge to protect the floor covering.

PAINTING WOODWORK

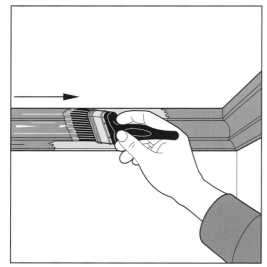

Painting ceiling moldings
Having primed, start in the corner with a 2-inch brush. Apply paint in the direction of the wood grain. Brush out with a wet brush and smooth without reloading it. At a new section, apply paint and brush back toward the wet edge. Feather the edge before moving to another section.

Painting intricate moldings
Use a stencil brush to fill the grooves and creases of elaborate molding designs. The round shape and closely spaced bristles of a stencil brush do a good job of forcing paint into every part of the design.

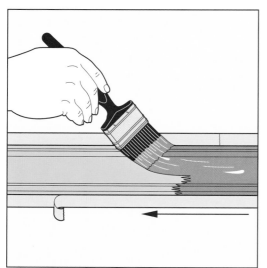

Painting chair-rail moldings
Be sure to protect the wall on both sides of the molding. For the narrow edges along the top and bottom, switch to a small pad or artist's brush. Paint these sections while the main part of the molding is wet. Smooth out drips before moving to another section.

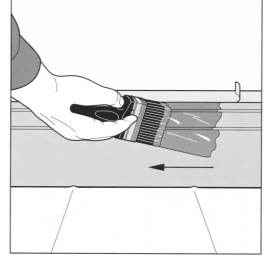

Painting baseboards
As with other woodwork, paint in the direction of the grain. Protect the floor with masking tape or heavy kraft paper.

AVOIDING LAP MARKS

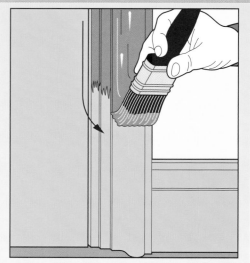

① Feather the edge
Lap marks show up more with a glossy paint. Since most woodwork is finished with a shiny surface, it is important to feather the edge. Brush the wood surface lightly with just the tips of the bristles, lifting the bristles as you reach the edge of a newly painted area.

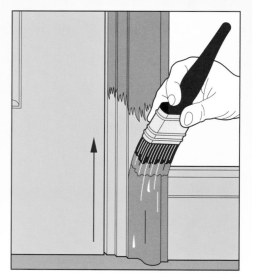

② Keep a wet edge on woodwork
Paint woodwork in small sections, keeping a wet edge to avoid lap marks. Apply new paint in a dry area and work back toward previously applied paint. Brush in the direction of the grain.

PAINTING SHELVES

Treat each shelf as a separate section. Complete an entire section before moving on to the next.

WORK SEQUENCE

1   Starting at the top shelf, paint the back wall of the bookcase.
2   Next, paint the sidewalls of the section you are working on.
3   Then paint the upper and lower shelf surfaces.
4   Complete the other sections in the same way.
5   Finally, paint the exposed horizontal and vertical edges.

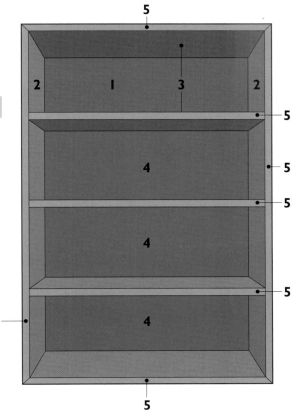

PAINTING SHELVES

A way to work on shelves without touching the wet paint is to remove them and drive nails part of the way through the edges of the shelves. Then rest the nails on sawhorses or old chairs (*p.89*), leaving the surface clear for painting.

STAINING WOODWORK

Apply the stain
Wear rubber gloves and protect the floors and walls by masking. Apply with a brush or a rag in the direction of the wood grain. Work in small sections so that you can control the level of stain penetration.

Wipe off the stain
Wait as directed on the label and then wipe off with a clean rag. As the work progresses, you will develop a sense of the time between application and wiping off. This will help you achieve an even finish.

STAINS

Stains add color to wood while allowing its natural grain pattern to show through. When staining, allow the liquid to seep into the wood and then wipe off the excess to achieve the desired finish. By themselves, most stains do not protect the wood. The stain must be covered with polyurethane or another clear varnish. However, there are products available that contain both a stain and a protective finish in one.

The final look of the piece will depend on two things: the color stain and your technique. Many stores have stain-color samples, or the color may be shown on the can. The shade you end up with will depend on how long you allow the stain to penetrate the wood. Practice on a section of woodwork to be hidden behind furniture or on scrap lumber that matches the wood in your home.

Doors

The typical home may contain a number of different types of doors: hollow-core, solid-core, panel, louver, sliding, or French. Although the painting technique differs for each type of door, they all must stand up to dirty hands, bumps, and the occasional kick. You therefore need to paint doors with a semigloss-type paint for maximum protection and to make cleaning easier.

It is easier to paint the door in place than to take it off its hinges. However, if the door sticks when you open or close it, now may be a good time to take it down. Sometimes, sticking is caused by the accumulation of paint from previous paint jobs. Fix the problem by removing the door and sanding the paint off.

If the door is brand-new, paint it before installing it. Check with the manufacturer about its recommendations for painting the top and bottom edges of the door. Generally, you paint the bottoms of only those doors that open to the outside or are exposed to wet floors. The convention is to leave the tops of wood doors unpainted to help prevent warping.

Removing doorknobs on interior doors Loosen screws on doorknobs. This will allow you to pull or unscrew the knob from the spindle. Remove other knobs in this way.

PROFESSIONAL TIP

If you are leaving the door up for painting, keep it open with a rolled-up newspaper or some other type of wedge. Place drop cloths or newspaper under the door to catch any drips.

PREPARING DOORS

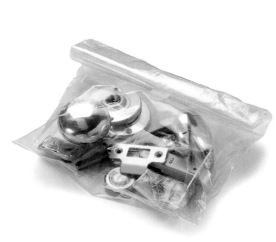

1 Remove doorknobs
Remove the screw that holds the knob to the stem. The protective plate around the stem should slip off unless it is held in place by a screw. Remove the screws from the latch plate and then pull out the assembly.

2 Mask around the doors
When painting doors, follow the directions for masking other types of woodwork (p.49). Protect adjoining walls with painter's tape. Make sure that the door is firmly wedged open.

REMOVING A DOOR

1 **Take the door off its hinges**
Close the door and use a screwdriver and hammer to remove the hinge pin. Keep tapping the pin until you can reach up and pull it free of the hinge barrel. Repeat for the bottom hinge or hinges. Remove the door from the opening.

2 **If the hinge won't budge**
If the hinge pin won't budge, blunt the head of a 2- or 3-inch common nail and insert it into the bottom of the hinge barrel. Then tap the nail head with a hammer until the pin pops free. Repeat for other hinges on the door if necessary.

REMOVING PAINT BUILDUP

Remove the door from its hinges and stand it on edge. Chip away at the old paint with a putty knife or single-edge razor. Follow up with a coarse-grit sandpaper and then a fine-grit paper until the edge is smooth. Then paint the door and replace it.

PAINTING REMOVED DOORS

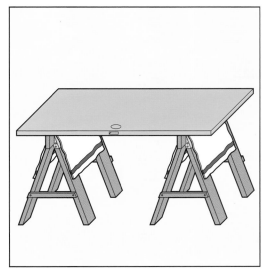

Lay the door across sawhorses
If you are removing the door, lay it across two sawhorses for painting. Cover the tops of the sawhorses with old towels to protect the finish of the door. Paint one side of the door (p.90), wait until it is dry, flip the door, and then paint the other side.

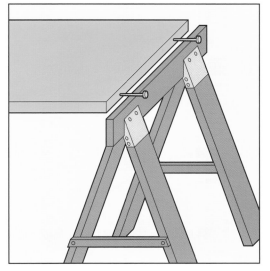

An alternative method
To continue painting before one side is dry, drive two nails into the top edge of the door and two nails into the bottom. Rest the nails on the sawhorses. With the aid of a helper, use the nails to turn the door over. Don't use this method on very heavy doors.

FIXING DOORS THAT STICK

There are many reasons why doors stick. The screws in the hinges may be loose, so check them and tighten them, if necessary. If the bottom of the door scrapes against the floor, you should trim it. To trim the door accurately, first mark the portion of the door that scrapes. Then remove the door from its hinges. Plane it with a small block plane or a power plane. Do not plane beyond the marked area. Finally, paint the door before you replace it.

PAINTING DOORS

Since doors are such a visible part of any room, take pains to apply a smooth, even finish. Help prevent lap marks by painting the entire door in one session. Begin by preparing the surface of the door as shown on pages 81–84. Prime as needed.

Painting each side a different color Most people simply paint the doors in a room the same color as the rest of the woodwork. If the door separates two rooms with different color woodwork, each side gets a coat of the appropriate color. The latch edge is painted the same color as the room into which the door opens.

Simple enough, but what guides your color selection if this is an interior door that is usually kept open? The best solution then is to paint the door a separate accent color, one that harmonizes with the colors in the adjoining rooms.

PROFESSSIONAL TIP

When you paint a door, leave enough time to paint the jambs and the hinge edge of the door first. Allow the jambs to dry before you paint the face and latch edges of the door. You can then close the door halfway without spoiling the finish on the inside jamb. Also, you won't ruin the finish or your clothes if you accidently brush against the latch jamb.

FLUSH DOORS

Generally, flush doors offer a solid, unbroken surface for painting. They can be made of either solid-core or hollow-core construction.

WORK SEQUENCE

1 **Start in the upper-left corner and paint an area extending about half of the way along the top of the door and a quarter of the way down.**

2 **Paint the adjoining section.**
3 **Follow the sequence shown on the diagram to finish painting the rest of the door.**

PAINTING FLUSH DOORS

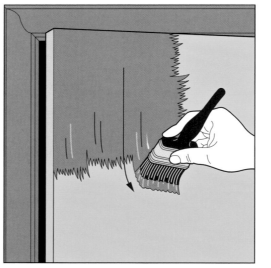

Lay on the paint
Load the bottom third of a 3-inch brush with paint. Start at the top of the door near the corner and paint the first section. Smooth the paint with horizontal strokes and then finish painting in the direction of the wood grain.

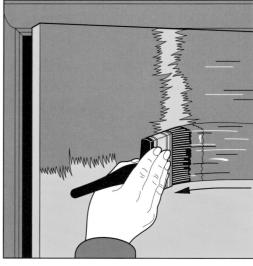

Feather the edge
Follow the feathering technique described on page 38. Begin the next portion of the door on a dry section and work toward the wet paint. Use a brush to smooth out any drips and beads that form along the edges, top, and bottom of the door.

USING A ROLLER

With a little practice, a roller will help you to make short work of flush doors.

Start in the middle

Work from the middle of the door to the top. Apply paint over the entire top half. Reload the roller and apply paint over the bottom half of the door.

Smooth with a brush

Use a brush to smooth out the finish. Paint from the top of the door down in long, even strokes.

PANEL DOORS

Panel doors have a more distinctive appearance than flush doors and require a little more care when painted. To paint panel doors, proceed as follows:

WORK SEQUENCE

1 Paint the panels first.
2 Paint the central vertical section, or stile, if there is one.
3 Paint the top horizontal rail.
4 Paint the middle horizontal rail.
5 Paint the other vertical stiles.
6 Finally, paint the bottom part of the door.

PAINTING A PANEL DOOR

Painting the panels

Load a 2-inch brush with paint and begin on the molding that surrounds one of the panels. Then paint the interior of the panel. Brush paint across the grain for even coverage, but always end by following the grain of the wood.

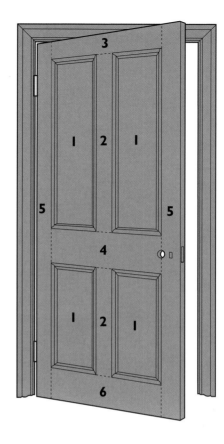

Painting the stiles and rails

Once you have painted the panels, paint the rest of the door in the sequence shown in the diagram above. Brush paint in the direction of the wood grain. Work quickly. You should aim to complete the door while the paint is still wet.

SLIDING DOORS

Sliding doors and French doors should be painted in the same way as any other type of door. The important difference is that these doors usually contain a glass area that must be protected from paint. Mask as necessary. Paint the outside as well as the inside. Paint sliding doors clockwise as follows:

WORK SEQUENCE

1 Begin by painting one vertical edge.
2 Paint the top of the frame.
3 Go on to the other side and the bottom of the same door.
4 Move on to the other door in the sliding set.

PROFESSIONAL TIP

Keep the sliding section of the door open an inch or two until the paint dries thoroughly. If you close the door while the paint is still wet, it will stick later. Also, move the slider occasionally to prevent the paint from forming a seal where the door meets the top and bottom tracks.

LOUVER DOORS

Louver doors are usually found on closets. Unlike those of shutters, the slats are usually fixed. Since your aim is to completely cover the slats, paint the back side of the door first. This also helps you to catch any paint drips from the front. Use oil-based paint to delay the drying process. Experiment with using foam pads (p.29) for painting the slats.

To paint louver doors, proceed as follows:

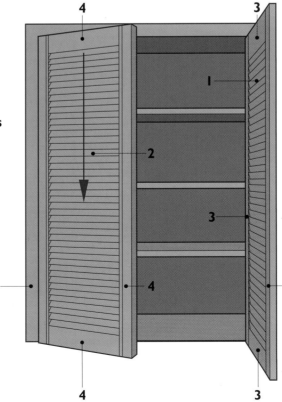

WORK SEQUENCE

1 Paint the back of the louvered section of the door. Work on one slat at a time from the top down. The method for painting each slat is shown on page 93.
2 Repeat the process for painting the louvers from the front of the door.
3 Then paint the top, sides, and bottom of the back of the door.
4 Finally, paint the top, sides, and bottom of the front of the door.

PAINTING SLATS ON FIXED LOUVERS

1 Work the paint into the crevices
Using a 1-inch brush, work the paint into the crevices between the slats of the louver. Paint from one edge toward the center of the slat. Be sure to paint the edge of the frame that holds the slats, but do not allow paint to accumulate there.

2 Brush the paint back
Flow the paint onto the wood in a long, smooth stroke. Start the next stroke at the opposite end of the same slat and flow the paint toward the wet area. Then smooth out the paint with horizontal strokes. Move on to the next slat down.

SPRAY PAINTING LOUVER DOORS

One way to ensure total coverage of door louvers is to use spray equipment. Take the door off its hinges and carry it outside. Then prop it against a wall or lay it over sawhorses. Be sure the area behind the door is protected from spray-through (paint going through the open louvers) and over-spray.

Holding the sprayer nozzle perpendicular to the surface (see p.42), paint the back of the door first, applying the paint in even strokes.

PAINTING ADJUSTABLE LOUVERS

1 Paint the edges of the frame
Open the louvers wide so that the slats are set horizontally. On the side of the door opposite the adjusting rod, use a 1-inch brush to paint the inside edges of the frame where the slats meet the frame.

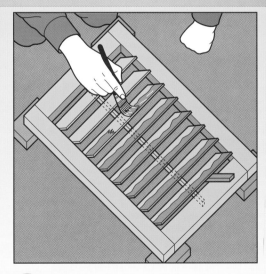

2 Paint both sides of the slats
Wedge a stick between the first slat and the frame, and paint the tops of both sides of the slats. Remove the stick, close the slats, and finish up unpainted areas of the slats. Then paint the frame.

3 Paint the other side of the door
On the other side of the door, paint the unpainted areas of the slats and the adjusting rod. Then paint the frame.

Windows

Windows come in a variety of shapes, sizes, and materials. Directions for preparing and painting double-hung, casements, and awnings are shown on the following pages. For other types, such as fixed, bow, and garden windows, follow the lead illustrated in the steps for painting the three main types: start to paint along the edge of the glass and work out to the casing.

We will deal with paintable wood window frames here, but you may have frames made of vinyl, aluminum, or fiberglass. You may even have frames made of two materials, such as wood with a cladding that you do not have to paint.

As with other woodwork, window frames should be painted with a gloss paint to protect the surface and make the windows easier to clean. When working, take care not to make the common error of smearing paint onto window glass. In order to avoid this mistake, make sure that you paint window frames in the proper sequence *(p.96 and p.98)*. Allow the paint to dry completely before closing the windows.

Opening a painted shut window There is no single way to open a stuck window, but there is a wrong way—the method that results in breaking the glass. No matter which technique you try, proceed slowly and carefully. Start with the simplest solution and work your way up to the most drastic *(p.95)*.

Preparing windows Clean window frames with a household cleanser to remove dirt and grease. Don't bother cleaning the glass until you are finished painting.

Preparing new windows Sand the rough spots on unpainted windows and wipe with a tack cloth or damp rag. Allow to dry thoroughly. Apply a coat of primer to seal the surface. Sand and paint when this is dry *(pp.97–99)*.

Cleaning the surface Wipe down all of the wood with a tack cloth to remove sanding dust, or use a damp rag to clean off the wood. Allow the surface to dry before painting.

Protecting the glass It is best to mask glass when painting windows *(p.49)*. However, with a little practice and concentration, it is possible to paint windows without masking. If you do paint without masking, keep a clean rag handy for removing any wet paint from the glass.

REPLACING BROKEN GLASS

To replace broken glass properly, follow these basic steps:

- Remove all broken glass and buy a new sheet that is 1/8-inch smaller than the length and width of the glass opening.
- Use a wire brush to clean out the rabbet, or notch, that holds the glass.
- Apply primer or linseed oil to the rabbet.
- Roll out a thin bead of glazing compound and place it in the rabbet. The compound will act as a bed for the new glass. Set the glass in place.
- Position glazier's points against the glass and force them into the wood with a putty knife. Install a point every 6 inches along the edge of the glass.
- Form some compound into a rope and press it against the edge of the glass. Starting in a corner, take a completely clean putty knife, hold it at about a 40-degree angle, and smooth out all of the compound until you reach another corner. Work in one continuous motion. Carefully scrape away any leftover compound. When you have finished, give the compound about one week to cure properly before painting.

OPENING A PAINTED SHUT WINDOW

Use a screwdriver

If the windows operate by a sash cord, the sashes—the part of the window that holds the glass—contain a channel for the cord. Insert a long screwdriver into the sash-cord channel and rock it back and forth. This may break the paint seal.

Cut the paint with a knife

An alternative method for opening a shut window is to try cutting through the paint seal with a sharp utility knife. Take care to cut only the dry paint and not to force the knife into the wood of the window frame.

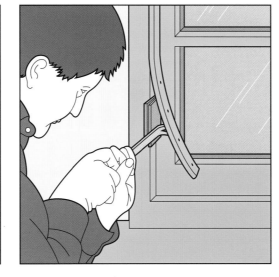

Use a putty knife and a hammer

If the screwdriver and the knife fail, work the corner of a putty knife between the sash and the window stop. Then insert as much of the blade as possible. Tap gently with a hammer to create an opening. Repeat the process all the way around the window.

Remove the window stop

A final solution calls for removing the window stop that holds the sash in place. Cut through the paint along the side of the stop with a utility knife and pry off the stop with a pry bar. Use cardboard or a wood block to protect the casing.

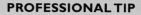

PROFESSIONAL TIP

The best brush to use on windows is a 2-inch angled sash brush. With the bristles forming an angle, you can get the paint into corners, and you'll find the brush easy to handle on a window's many narrow surfaces.

PROFESSIONAL TIP

When painting windows, allow a thin line of paint—about 1/8 inch—to overlap onto the glass. This will help keep moisture from working its way under the paint film.

PREPARING WINDOWS FOR PAINTING

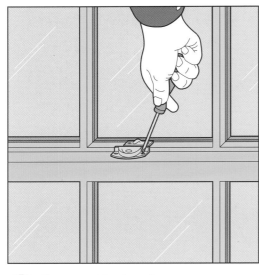

1 Remove the hardware
Remove all hardware, such as window handles and locks, and place in a plastic bag. If they are covered with old paint, soak the parts in the appropriate solvent to remove the paint.

2 Fill any holes
Use glazing compound or wood filler to fill all holes in the wood. Apply filler with a putty knife and smooth even with the surface of the wood. Allow to dry thoroughly. Sand if needed and spot prime.

3 Sand painted windows
Use a fine-grit sandpaper to roughen the surface of painted windows *(p.84)*. Tear the paper into thin strips for sanding the muntins. You can also use a liquid deglosser to dull the sheen.

SASH WINDOWS

Before beginning to paint sash windows, pull down the outer sash and lift the inner sash.

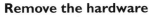

WORK SEQUENCE

1 Paint the outer sash muntins.
2 Paint the bottom and as much of the sides of the outer sash as you can reach.
3 Reverse the sash positions. Paint the rest of the outer sash.
4 Paint the inner sash.
5 When the paint is dry, push both sashes down and paint the upper jambs. When the upper jambs are dry, push the sashes up and paint the lower jambs, then the casing.

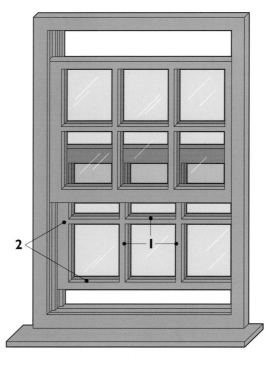

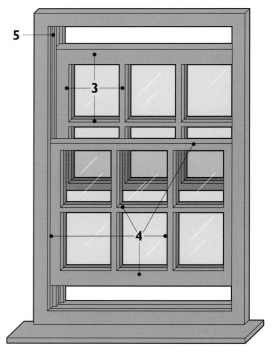

PAINTING SASH WINDOWS

1 **Paint the muntin**
Push the inner sash up and lower the outer sash. Paint the muntin on the outer sash. Hold the brush as you would a pencil. With the longest bristles facing up, flex the brush against the wood and draw the brush along the muntin/glass edge.

2 **Paint the bottom and sides of the outer sash**
Next, paint the bottom and sides of the outer sash. Apply paint as far up the sides of the sash as you can reach.

3 **Reverse the sashes**
Move the inner sash down to within an inch of being closed and raise the outer sash to about an inch from the top. Paint the rest of the outer sash.

4 **Paint the inner sash**
Paint the entire inner sash. Don't close the sashes until the paint is dry. While waiting for the paint to dry, move the sashes up and down a few inches every so often in order to break any paint seals that may be forming.

5 **Paint the jambs**
When the sashes are completely dry (wait at least 24 hours), push both sashes all the way down. Paint the upper half of the jambs. Allow to dry completely, then push the sashes up and paint the lower half. Paint the stops and then the casing.

PAINTING WINDOW JAMBS

Paint the lower window jambs the same color as the interior woodwork. Paint the upper jamb the same color as the exterior woodwork. Using this method allows you to match color schemes, whether you are viewing the window from the inside or the outside of the house.

CASEMENT WINDOWS

To paint casement windows, proceed as follows:

WORK SEQUENCE

1 Open the window and paint the edge of the frame where it meets the glass.
2 Paint the top of the window frame.
3 Next, paint the bottom and sides of the window.
4 Then paint the window jambs.
5 Finally, paint the casing.

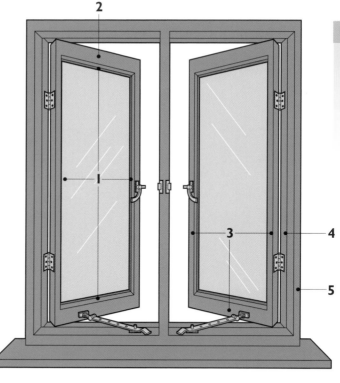

PROFESSIONAL TIP

Metal Windows
Clean the windows and remove rust with a wire brush. Prime with a metal primer before painting. Paint as shown on pages 97–99.

PROFESSIONAL TIP

Many painters get good results by using small rollers or painting pads rather than brushes on window frames. Use rollers on the wider sections of frames. Painting pads have tapered edges that do a good job on muntins. Pads work well with water-based paints, but some oil-based paints will damage the rubber in them.

PAINTING CASEMENT WINDOWS

Paint the casement
Open the windows and begin at the top of the casement. Start by painting the edge along the glass and, working outward, paint in the direction of the wood grain. Paint the bottom and sides. When painting multipane windows, start with the muntins.

Paint the jambs
Paint the jambs once the casement has had time to dry. While the paint is drying, crank the window open or closed a little to break any paint seal that may be forming. Avoid getting paint on the hinges.

AWNING WINDOWS

This type of window is similar to a casement turned on its side. Paint in the same manner as for casements.

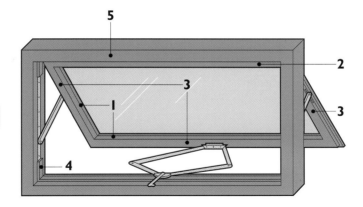

WORK SEQUENCE

1 Open the window and paint the edge of the frame where it meets the glass.
2 Paint the top of the window frame.
3 Next, paint the bottom and sides of the window.
4 Then paint the window jambs.
5 Finally, paint the casing.

REMOVING PAINT FROM GLASS

- Use a clean cloth to wipe up any paint that finds its way onto the glass.
- Wrap a cloth around the blade of a putty knife to clean up paint along the edge of the glass.

- If you miss some spots, leave the paint until it is dry to the touch and then scrape it off with a single-edge razor.

TO AVOID MASKING WINDOWPANES

1 Overlap the glass with paint
Rather than masking, allow your brush to overlap the glass slightly. Keep the overlap small, and concentrate on applying the paint smoothly over the frame. Wait until the paint is dry to the touch but not cured completely.

2 Score the paint
At this stage, the paint will still appear to be wet, although you won't be able to smudge it with your finger. Using a straightedge and a single-edge razor, score a line through the paint on the glass about $1/16$ to $1/8$ of an inch from the frame.

3 Scrape away the excess
Using a single-edge razor or razor knife, scrape the paint from the glass up to the score line. This should give the window frame a crisp painted edge. Allow the paint to dry completely before you wash the windows.

Painted finishes on walls and cabinets can enhance and soften the hard metal and tile surfaces usually found in kitchens and bathrooms. But because these rooms get a great deal of use and inevitably collect grease and dirt, the paint must be both washable and able to stand up to the water vapor generated by cooking and bathing.

CHAPTER 7

KITCHENS AND BATHROOMS

The surfaces

Begin work on kitchens and bathrooms by performing the preparatory chores you would normally do in any room: scraping loose paint and repairing damage to ceilings and walls *(pp.58–68)*. Your thoroughness in cleaning the walls and other surfaces is especially important here. In some cases you may have to scrape away layers of grease or soap film that has managed to build up in some out-of-the-way spot. Check behind the cooking range, on the walls around ventilation hoods, and around in-wall ventilation fans. Be sure that you remove all of the grease because paint applied to any kind of surface film will not bond correctly.

You must also decide whether you want to paint the cabinets in these rooms. If the cabinets are in good condition and work well with the color scheme of the room, it is probably best to leave them as they are. Just be sure they are well protected while you paint the walls and ceilings around them. You can either paint or replace any damaged or shabby cabinets.

New cabinets enhance the appearance of the room and may provide you with more storage options than the old cabinets did. However, new cabinets can be expensive. So if it is the finish you want to change, not the inside of the cabinets, consider painting or staining them. A new color along with some new cabinet and drawer pulls and knobs will refresh and update even the most worn-out looking kitchen.

When choosing a color for your cabinetry, remember that color will set the tone for the entire room. Choosing a very fashionable color may look great for a short time, but you may tire of living with it day after day. On the other hand, a neutral color will force something else to become the focus of the room.

MATERIALS AND TOOLS

Cleansers
Sponges and nonscratch scouring pads
Paint scrapers
Drywall saw
Sandpaper
Screwdriver
Painter's tape
Drop cloths (canvas and plastic)
Brushes and rollers
Primer
Paint

IMPROVING VENTILATION

The moisture that builds up in kitchens and bathrooms should be vented outside. Water vapor that condenses on walls and other surfaces can lead to peeling paint, mildew, and, in extreme cases, structural damage. Most new houses contain some kind of mechanical ventilation, but older homes often do not. In addition to windows, a kitchen should have a ventilating fan mounted in a range hood. A bathroom should have an exhaust fan installed in the wall or the ceiling. New models that include both a light fixture and a fan are available. Consult a contractor who specializes in kitchens and bathrooms for proper sizing of the fan and installation.

Kitchens

Protecting kitchens When you set out to paint your kitchen, you will notice how little of the room needs painting. This means that there are far more surfaces, including counters, appliances, and cabinets, to protect from splattered paint.

Covering appliances Move appliances—with the exception of the gas range—to the center of the room and cover with drop cloths. You should also cover the floor with drop cloths.

Removing hardware Remove cabinet and drawer pulls by unscrewing them from the inside. Place all hardware and screws in a plastic bag until it is time to reinstall them.

Cleaning walls Clean off grease with either a household detergent or trisodium phosphate. A sponge or nonabrasive scouring pad will clean off grime. Remove mildew with a solution of one quart of chlorine bleach to three quarts of water.

Work areas If the kitchen is small, you will probably have to use a counter or a tabletop as your main work area for mixing and pouring paint. Cover with drop cloths and, to protect against paint-can scratches, use a few layers of old newspapers.

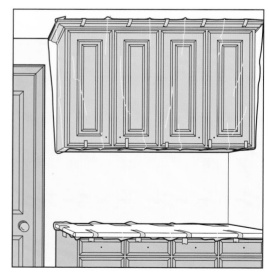

MOVING LARGE APPLIANCES

Kitchens usually contain large appliances and sometimes big pieces of furniture, such as sideboards, that must be moved away from the wall. Since these items are usually heavy and awkward, walk them rather than lift them. Begin by moving one corner of the appliance a few inches and then do the same to the opposite corner. Although this method takes time, at least you will avoid injuring yourself. Protect your floor from scratches by walking heavy appliances onto a piece of thick cardboard or old carpeting turned upside down.

PREPARING KITCHENS

Move appliances away from the wall
When appliances can't be placed in the center of the room, because the room is small or has a center island, move the range and refrigerator far away enough from the wall to allow you to paint behind them.

Protect the cabinets
If you are not going to paint your cabinets, hang a sheet of plastic (polyethylene film) over them. Secure with masking tape at the top and sides. If you do plan on painting them later, don't bother masking them.

PAINTING KITCHEN CEILINGS AND WALLS

Before painting unpainted walls and ceilings, you must apply a coat of primer (*p.24*). It isn't necessary to prime previously painted walls if you have removed all of the grease buildup. If you aren't certain whether a surface is absolutely clean, apply primer.

Use a high-sheen paint, such as a semigloss, that can stand up to repeated washings. Many manufacturers have introduced paints that are specially formulated for use in kitchens and bathrooms. These products contain a mildewcide that will help to prevent mildew from forming on the finish. They can also stand up to the high levels of water vapor common in these rooms.

Paint in the same order as that for any other room: first the ceiling, next the walls, then the woodwork, and finally the cabinets.

PAINTING KITCHEN CABINETS

There are two decisions you must make before painting kitchen cabinets: should you paint the insides of the cabinets, and should you leave the doors on or take them off?

Unless the cabinets have glass doors, don't bother to paint the insides. Kitchen cabinets usually remain closed; even when they are open, whatever is stored inside usually hides the walls. With base cabinets, you must bend over or squat down to see inside. Of course, it may bother you to see unpainted interiors every time you open a cabinet door. If you decide to paint them, follow the painting sequence on page 104.

If you are considering whether to remove the cabinet doors, follow these basic guidelines:

- Don't remove the doors if you are simply going to sand and paint them. However, you may find it easier to remove the doors than to paint around exposed hinges.
- Remove the doors if you plan to install new exposed hinges.
- Remove the doors if you are going to strip the old finish. This will allow you to apply a chemical stripper in the basement or garage or outside. Follow the directions for stripping woodwork on pages 82–83.

Make sure that you get good results on your old cabinets by choosing the best-quality primer and paint available. It is also a good idea to use new brushes and to invest in tack cloths for removing sanding dust.

PREPARING KITCHEN CABINETS

Prepare kitchen cabinets carefully before painting them. Use a fine-grit sandpaper to sand the inside and outside of the cabinet doors and drawers. Sand the frame of the cabinet. This removes imperfections and provides a good base for the primer. Wipe up the dust with a tack cloth. Apply a coat of primer.

SAFETY FOR GAS RANGES

Always be careful if you have to move a gas range. You will be unable to move ranges that are connected to your home's gas line by a pipe. If the range is attached by flexible tubing, use a flashlight to see how much slack there is behind the appliance. It is better to leave the range in place than to risk stretching the tubing too tautly. If the wall behind or beside the range is visible and must be painted, use a small roller attached to an extension handle.

COLORS FOR KITCHENS

The main consideration for any kitchen is that it should be both functional and bright. This is why one of the most popular colors for kitchens has been white with a contrasting color like blue or yellow. Nowadays, however, many people are choosing more dramatic or fashionable colors to make the color scheme in the kitchen just as interesting as in the other rooms in a house. These colors often work well because, if you choose bland, neutral colors, you may well find that such objects as a refrigerator and a cooking range may seem to dominate the room.

KITCHEN CABINETS

If you want to paint the insides of a cabinet, follow the sequence shown on page 87. If you want to paint only the outside of a cabinet, proceed as follows:

WORK SEQUENCE

1 Paint the inside, then the outside, of the doors.
2 Next, paint the horizontal sections of the frame.
3 Then, paint the vertical sections, or stiles, of the frame.
4 Finally, paint the outer sides of the cabinets.

PAINTING UNDER WALL CABINETS

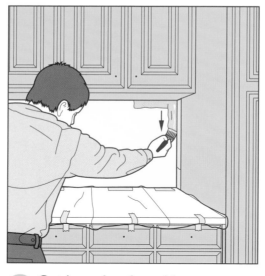

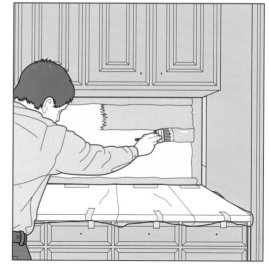

1 Cut in under the cabinets
Use a 2-inch brush to cut in under the cabinets. In most cases, you will be able to use the bottom edge of the wall cabinets as a guide. Painting this area can be awkward, as you must bend and reach across the counter to get to the wall.

2 Lay on and smooth the paint and feather the edge
Cover the rest of the area with a 3-inch brush. Then lay on and smooth the paint and feather the edge *(p.38)*. Work in sections that span the distance between the bottom of the cabinets and the counter.

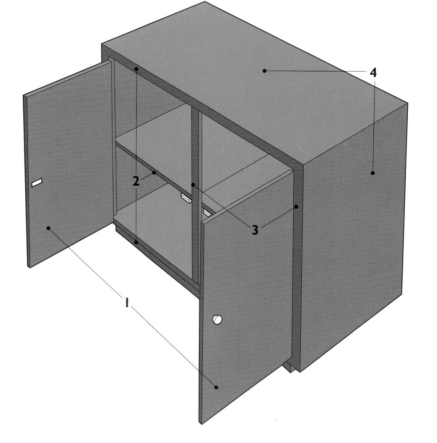

PAINTING KITCHEN CABINETS

1 Paint the doors

Use a new 3-inch brush to paint the inside of the door, using your free hand to hold the door in position. Don't forget to paint the hinge-side edge of the door. Allow the paint to dry before closing the door. Then paint the outside of the door.

2 Paint the horizontal sections

Use a 2-inch brush to paint the horizontal sections of the cabinet frame. Don't forget to paint the front of the cabinet shelves.

3 Paint the vertical sections

Next, paint the vertical sections of the cabinet. Be sure to go over your work and correct any paint drips or runs that may have occurred.

4 Paint the sides

Finish by painting any exposed sides of the cabinet. These normally occur where neighboring cabinets are of different depths or at the end of a run of cabinets.

GETTING NEW HARDWARE

Consider installing new cabinet hardware to complete the job you started by painting the cabinets. Replace pulls with pulls and knobs with knobs because the holes needed for installation are already in place. If you do change the hardware, fill any holes that won't be used before painting and drill any new holes after painting. Use a level for installing pulls.

Bathrooms

Preparing bathrooms Unlike other rooms in the house, bathrooms rarely have movable furniture, and most pieces will have to be protected as directed below. Any furniture that can be moved should be removed and stored elsewhere until the job is completed.

Scrape loose paint and make any repairs to walls and woodwork as necessary. If mildew is present, remove it with a solution of one part chlorine bleach to three parts water.

Painting bathrooms A high-sheen paint will make the bathroom easier to clean. Also consider using one of the paints that are formulated to withstand the high levels of moisture found in every bathroom.

Choosing painted or tiled surfaces Ceramic tiles that can be easily washed may seem like a good solution for bathrooms (and many kitchens). However, bathrooms, even more so than kitchens, tend to have recesses, ledges, and pipes that cannot be tiled. It is best to paint these areas, especially as there are now paints on the market that are formulated to cope with high-moisture conditions.

DEALING WITH WATER DAMAGE

Water damage in bathrooms can be caused by leaky pipes, splatter from showers and tubs, and condensation on the walls. To avoid future damage, correct the source of the problem before beginning to paint *(p.59)*. Deal with water spots by coating them with a primer containing shellac.

MAINTAINING THE PAINT JOB

Keep your paint job looking like new by ensuring proper ventilation in the room. If necessary, wipe down walls with a dry cloth or towel to remove condensation.

Regularly clean soap scum off the walls with a bathroom cleaner.

PROTECTING BATHROOM FIXTURES

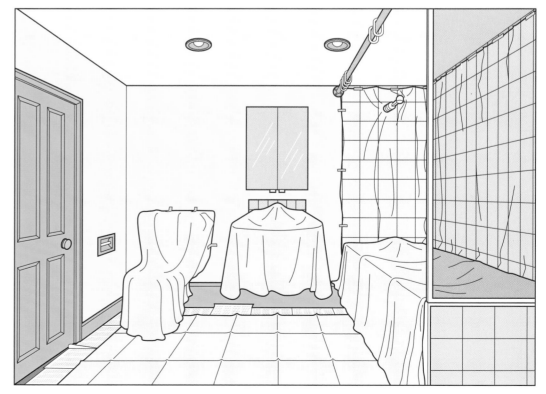

Protect parts of the bathroom that won't be painted

Cover any unpainted areas of the bathroom, such as the toilet and the vanity mirror, with a drop cloth. Tape plastic sheets over tile walls. Use drop cloths on floors. Protect the tub by taping the drop cloth over it.

PROTECTING BATHROOM FIXTURES

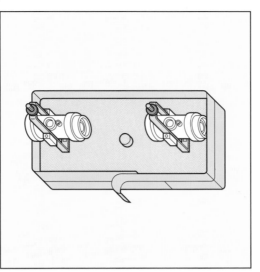

Cover the faucets
Keep paint drips and splatters off faucets and spouts by constructing newspaper hoods. First, fold a sheet of paper to form a semicircle and then attach it to the wall with painter's tape.

Protect the light fixtures
Remove the globe and bulbs. Apply painter's tape around the edges of the fixture. For extra light while you are working, keep light bulbs in place on the opposite wall.

PAINTING BATHROOMS

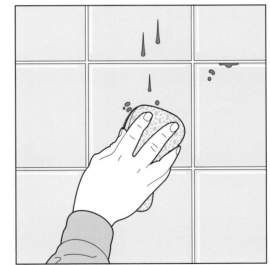

Painting around the medicine cabinet
Having masked the edges with painter's tape, use a 2-inch brush to apply the paint. Paint around the medicine cabinet in the same way that you would paint around a window. Keep a clean cloth handy to wipe up any paint splatters that land on the cabinet.

Painting around a light fixture
Use a 2-inch brush to paint around a light fixture. If you kept the bulbs in place and lights on when painting other parts of the room, remove the bulbs now. If you keep them in place, their glare will prevent you from seeing what you are painting clearly.

Clean up spills on tiles
Wipe up spills immediately. If you miss any, let the spill dry completely and then rub it off with a nonabrasive scouring pad.

Some areas of the home present special challenges and should be dealt with differently from the rest of the painting project. In this chapter you'll find directions for refinishing floors and painting stairs, stairwells, pipes, and masonry surfaces. These areas are important parts of your home and should be given the same attention as walls and ceilings. You will learn how to tackle these jobs and achieve good results.

CHAPTER 8

SPECIAL SITUATIONS

Stairs and stairwells

Although they may not take up a great deal of space, both stairs and stairwells require special treatment. A staircase is often the focal point in a home. Even a house that otherwise has little ornamentation may have an attractive staircase, meant to be the center of attention. Thus, the stairs should be restored and painted with care.

In most houses the stairs are in almost constant use by family members. So it is important to learn how to paint stairs while allowing people to use them. This will require careful timing and working in a specific sequence.

Staining or painting In many older homes, stairs were built with high-quality woods that were originally stained rather than painted. If your stairs are painted and the house contains ornate moldings in other areas, the stairs may have decorative elements too, and you may consider stripping and staining them. Choose an inconspicuous part of the stairs and scrape off the paint. If there is a buildup of layers of old paint, you will have to use a chemical stripper to remove the finish down to the bare wood. A carpenter should be able to identify the wood and advise you on the feasibility of stripping all the stairs. It may not be worth stripping and staining stairs if they are made of low-quality wood.

Choosing paint It is usually best to choose for a staircase wall the same paint sheen you selected for other walls in the house. But consider using a more washable sheen if the staircase walls have become dirty because people touch them as they use the stairs. You can avoid this problem, and increase safety, by installing a handrail on the wall.

Special equipment The high walls and ceilings of stairwells present their own set of challenges. You'll need special ladder and scaffold setups to paint stairwells *(p.111)*. Retractable stepladders, which allow you to adjust the height of each leg independently, come in handy for setting up on stairs. You may also need a straight ladder, of the type that is usually used for outdoor work, to anchor one side of the scaffold. A roller extension will also help you to reach the ceiling and tops of the high walls in a stairwell.

MATERIALS AND TOOLS

Stains and paints
Ladders
Stepladders
Scaffold planks
Brushes, rollers, and roller extensions
Heavy paper or painter's tape

WORKING ON STAIRCASES

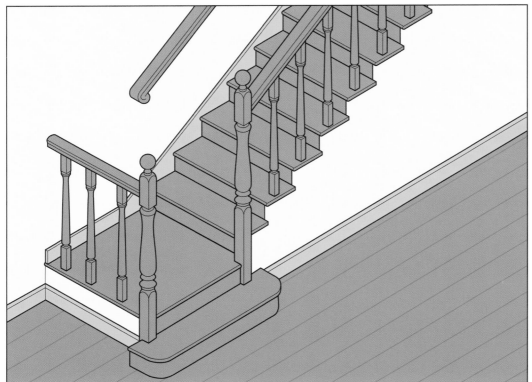

The parts of a staircase

Even if the steps are covered with carpeting, you will still need to paint the stairwell and the balustrade, which includes the newel post, handrail, and balusters of the railing. If you are adding a new railing, consider the reach of the elderly and children when deciding on a height for the handrail. One option is to install a double-height handrail to accommodate everyone in the family.

PROFESSIONAL TIP

As an alternative to the method of painting steps shown below, paint alternate steps. Allow them to dry, then paint the other steps.

PAINTING STAIRS

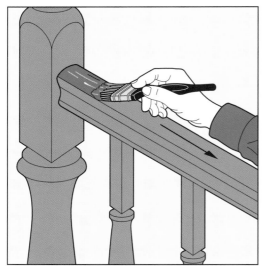

1 Paint the handrail first

Place drop cloths on the steps to protect against spills and begin by painting the balustrade. Use a narrow brush to apply paint or stain in the direction of the wood grain. Start at the top of the handrail and work toward the bottom of the stairs.

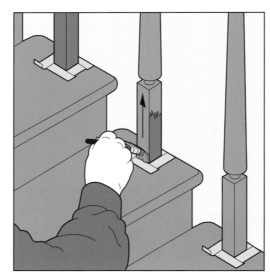

2 Paint the balusters

After masking around the base of the balusters with heavy paper or painter's tape, paint the balusters. Brush from the bottom up. Smooth out the paint on each baluster to remove drips before moving on. Replace the tape when it begins to pick up paint.

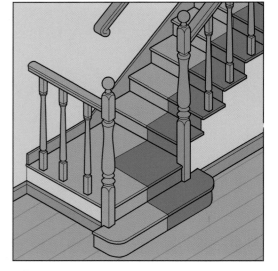

3 Paint the steps

If the stairs are in use while you are painting, paint half the width of each step and allow to dry. Paint the riser and the tread of each step, then paint the overhang. When the painted portion is dry, paint the other half of each step.

WORKING IN STAIRWELLS

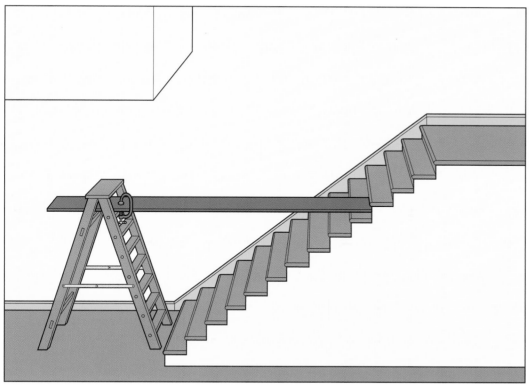

Scaffolding for the lower stairwell

For lower areas you may be able to use scaffolding with only a stepladder. Place the scaffold between the stepladder in the hall and one of the steps on the staircase. As you paint, move the scaffold down the stepladder rungs and the staircase steps.

PROFESSIONAL TIP

Make sure that your scaffold setup is safe. Ladders' steps should face toward the scaffold plank. This will provide the scaffolding with adequate support. Clamp the scaffolding to the ladder. Also, check the stepladder braces from time to time to make sure that they are locked and tight.

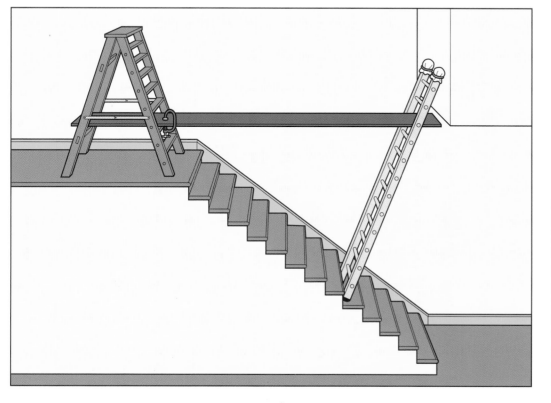

Scaffolding for the upper stairwell

For high areas you will need a straight ladder and a stepladder. Place the scaffold between the stepladder at the top of the staircase and the straight ladder that is propped up against the wall. You can prevent the straight ladder from marking the wall by wrapping the top of the ladder with towels or by placing special rubber pads over the ends. To make it safe, the scaffold should overlap the ladder rungs by at least 12 inches.

Floors

Almost every kind of floor covering can be painted. This section deals with preparing, painting, and refinishing wood floors and preparing and painting concrete floors.

Use only those paints that have been specially designed for covering floors and decks. Standard paints cannot withstand the amount of wear and tear that floors have to undergo as well as a good-quality floor paint can. Floor paints are available in both oil- and water-based formulations.

Wood floors can be stained to allow the grain of the wood to show through and then covered with a clear protective finish. There are two main types of finishes: clear varnishes and wax finishes. The most popular clear varnishes are oil- or water-based polyurethanes and urethanes. They are relatively easy to apply and are available in a variety of sheens. Nowadays, few people opt for a wax finish, but you may have to deal with a wax finish when stripping or repairing an old floor.

Whatever finish you decide on for your floor, you should begin the project by preparing the surface properly. You may need to make repairs, and you will have to strip off the old finish before applying paint or varnish.

MATERIALS AND TOOLS

Paints and primers
Clear finishes
Stain and thinner
Rollers, roller extensions, brushes, and paint pads
Steel wool
Pry bar
Hammer and nail set
Power screwdriver
Carpenter's glue
Chisel
Sanding machines
Rotary buffing machines
Handheld scrapers
Sandpaper
Buffing pads
Patching concrete

REPAIRING DAMAGED FINISHES

A wood floor that is showing its age because of damage or wear should be completely refinished or repainted. But if the scuffs and scratches are not severe, you may be able to make spot repairs and prolong the life of the existing finish.

To find out which type of finish is on the floor, conduct a simple test. A wax finish will smudge when you press against it with your finger. You will also be able to remove some wax by scraping the surface with the edge of a coin. If the surface flakes up in pieces rather than producing a waxy residue, the finish is varnish.

If you have to repair an area that has been colored with a stain, choose one that matches the color of the rest of the floor most closely. Use a piece of wood of the same type as your floor to experiment with different ratios of stain to thinner until you match the color satisfactorily.

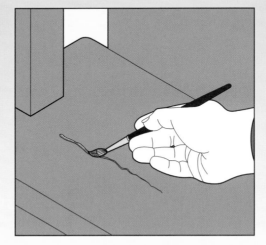

Scratches in a polyurethane finish
Using a finish that matches the existing sheen, apply polyurethane varnish with an artist's brush. Wipe up varnish that drips on other parts of the floor. You can buy kits for small repairs on this type of finish.

Scratches in a wax finish
First of all, buff the scratched area with a clean cloth. If the damage is still there, buff once more with extra-fine steel wool. When finished, apply a light coating of wax to the damaged area and buff again.

STAIN OR PAINT

The natural grain of wood has an attractive pattern that is generally allowed to show through the finish of a wood floor. Usually, wood floors are treated with a light stain or left natural, with a clear, protective finish completing the job. But there are some cases in which you may consider painting over a natural-wood floor. A rich, opaque color may suit your overall decorating scheme better than a clear finish does. Or it may be that the floor is so badly damaged, or made from such an inferior wood, that it is unsightly and would be best covered with paint.

It is possible to combine paint with traditional, clear-finish products on the same floor. Some professional designers decorate a wood floor by stenciling a painted design on the floor. Another method of decoration is to paint a border around the edges of a room while staining the rest of the floor.

Preparing wood floors for finishing Whether you are painting or staining your wood floor, you must begin by making the necessary repairs. These preparations may include replacing wood plugs, fixing warped planks *(p.114)*, or removing and replacing damaged boards *(p.115)*. It may be necessary to sand a wood floor, especially if you intend to stain or apply a clear finish to the floor *(pp.116–117)*. However, make sure that before sanding, you countersink all protruding nail heads, using a hammer and nail set. This helps to secure the planks to the floor and prevents the nails from ripping sandpaper.

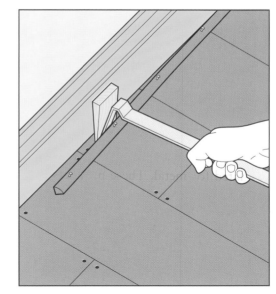

Removing the base shoe
Gently pry off the base shoe, the narrow strip of molding installed at the bottom of the baseboard. Wedge a thin piece of wood or heavy cardboard between the baseboard and the pry bar to protect the finish. Removing the base shoe allows you to sand and apply finish right up to the edge of the wall. When the base shoe is reinstalled, it will hide any rough edges around the perimeter of the room.

FLOOR FINISHES

Type of finish	Color	Drying time	Sheen
Paint	Limited selection	Fast	Satin to gloss
Oil-based polyurethane	Amber when dry	Slow	Satin to gloss
Water-based urethane	Clear	Fast	Satin to gloss
Seal and wax	Amber	Slow	Wax shine

BASE SHOES
Some antique base shoes have decorative finishes. It is worth taking care to avoid damaging them, so that you can reuse them. Most softwood moldings are relatively inexpensive to replace, so don't be upset if the shoe splits during removal. It is best to devote your time to protecting the finish on the baseboard.

REPLACING WOOD PLUGS

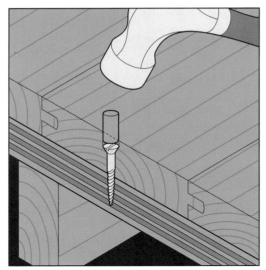

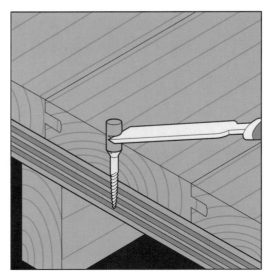

1 Tap the dowels into holes
Some floors have plugs that hide screw heads. If you cannot find replacements for missing plugs, use hardwood dowels. Coat the sides of the dowel with carpenter's glue and tap it into the hole.

2 Cut the dowel
When the glue dries, cut the part of the dowel that sticks above the floor with a chisel or fine-tooth saw. Sand the dowel even with the floor. Then stain it to match the rest of the floor.

FIXING WARPED PLANKS

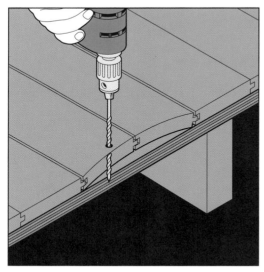

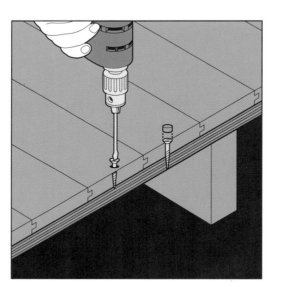

1 Drill pilot holes
Realign warped planks by screwing them back into position. First, drill pilot holes, slightly smaller than the screws, every 3 or 4 inches along the damaged area. The screws should be about 1/4 inch shorter than the thickness of the plank and subfloor.

2 Screw back into position
Drive wood screws into the holes. This will pull the plank back. If more than one plank is buckled, work from the edges of the damaged area toward the center. Hide the repair by countersinking the screws and covering with wood plugs.

PROFESSIONAL TIP

Woods absorb stains in a different way from one another. If you cannot find wood plugs made of the same material as your floor, you will need to find a stain formulation that makes the new plug match the floor. Experiment with formulations on a test piece of wood. Allow the stain to dry thoroughly to find an exact match.

WORKING ON PLANKS FROM UNDERNEATH

If you have access to the underside of the wood floor, you may find that this is the easiest way to fix warped planks. Place a weight or have a helper stand on the damaged area of floor. Drill pilot holes and drive screws with metal washers through the subfloor and into the wood planks. This action should pull the wood back into its proper position.

REMOVING DAMAGED BOARDS

To remove a complete board
Remove a complete board that is damaged by splitting it with a wood chisel in a number of places. Then pry up the pieces. Remove nails with a claw hammer.

To remove part of a board
To remove the damaged section of a large board, drill a series of holes at each end of the damaged area. Square the edges with a wood chisel. Replace the board.

FIXING A SQUEAKY FLOOR

The noise of a squeaky floor is usually caused by one piece of wood rubbing against another. The rubbing must be eliminated to silence the noise. If the source of the problem is over a joist and you have access to the underside of the floor, apply carpenter's glue to a shim and drive it between the joist and the subfloor. If you have to work from above, drill pilot holes and drive screws or spiral-shank nails into the joist or the subfloor. Tightening up the connections usually eliminates the rubbing.

REPLACING A TONGUE-AND-GROOVE BOARD

1 Prepare the new board
Cut the new board to the correct length to fill the gap. Turn the board upside down and remove the bottom lip of the groove with a chisel.

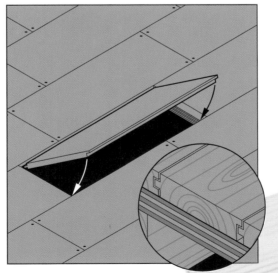

2 Glue the edges
Apply carpenter's glue to the edges of the tongue and the remaining part of the groove. Tip the section at an angle and insert the tongue into the groove of the adjoining plank.

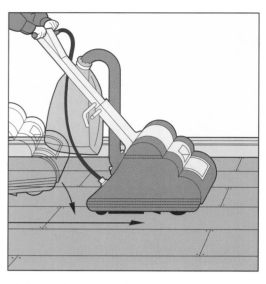

SANDING

If you plan to repaint a floor, simply prepare the surface by scraping away any loose paint and cleaning the floor. However, if you plan to apply a clear protective finish to a floor, you will have to sand away the existing finish first.

To sand a floor, you will need a drum sander, an edge sander, a rotary buffer, and various handheld scrapers. You can rent most of these tools—except for the handheld tools—from a tool-rental outlet or a flooring dealer. Describe the condition of the floor and its size to the rental agent. He will advise you about the type of machines, abrasives, and polishers you will need. Ask the agent to demonstrate how you should use the machines. You will also need sandpaper for the drum sander and edge sander, and steel wool or buffing pads for the rotary buffer.

Remember that a drum sander is a very powerful tool that can easily damage your floor if you are not careful. A rotary buffer can be difficult to use. Some buffers are operated with controls located on the handle. Others work by having the handle moved up and down, an action that takes some getting used to. It is important to keep moving, as buffing in one place for too long can remove too much of the finish.

Using a drum sander
Attach sandpaper to the drum, following the agent's directions. The key to using a drum sander is to make sure that you keep it moving when the sandpaper is in contact with the floor. Keep the sander in the up position when standing still and lower it as you move forward or backward.

Sanding the floor
Begin at one end of the room with the sander loaded with a rough-grit sandpaper and pointing in the direction in which the boards are laid. Always sand with the grain of the wood. Stand about two thirds of the distance from the wall. Turn the machine on with the sander raised off the floor, begin walking, and slowly lower the sander to the floor. As you get close to the opposite wall, raise the sander. Walk backward, lowering the sander into position while moving.

As you near your original starting point, raise the sander. Move the machine 4 or 5 inches to the side and begin a new pass. Sand the rest of the floor in this way. Then point the sander in the opposite direction and sand the remaining third of the room in the same manner. When you have finished, switch to a finer-grit sandpaper and begin the whole process over again.

SANDING DIFFICULT AREAS OF THE ROOM

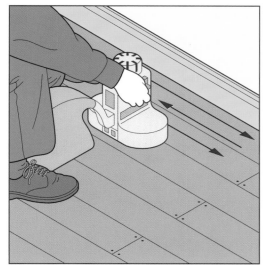

1 Guide the sander back and forth
Use an edge sander for areas against the wall. If the floor planks are parallel to the wall, guide the tool back and forth in the direction of the wood grain. Start with a rough-grit disk for the first pass. Follow with finer-grit disks.

2 Follow the grain of the wood
If the planks are perpendicular to the wall, guide the edge sander against the baseboard and then pull away in a half-circle motion. Overlap the areas sanded with the drum sander by four to six inches.

3 Sanding hard-to-reach areas
Use the handheld scraper to remove the finish from corners and other out-of-the-way areas. Pull the blade of the tool toward you. Follow by hand sanding with medium- and then fine-grit sandpaper attached to a sanding block.

SANDING PARQUET FLOORS

These floors present a special challenge because each parquet, or floor tile, is made up of a number of small pieces of wood set perpendicular to one another. As a result, special care must be taken to avoid leaving ugly cross-grain scratches on the surface when you sand.

To remove the finish from a parquet floor, sand in a diagonal direction. Use a rotary buffer and attach a medium-grit sandpaper. Make the first cut starting in one corner and work to the opposite corner. Sand the entire floor in this direction. Switch to a finer-grit paper and make the second pass on the opposite diagonal. Sand the entire floor. The final pass should be made parallel to the longest wall; use a buffer equipped with a sanding disk.

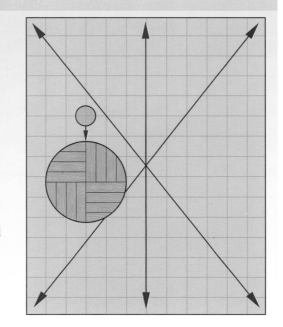

SANDING SAFELY

Sanding produces wood dust that can be highly combustible. Power sanders come equipped with a bag to catch most of the wood dust produced by sanding. Still, some dust will escape, so wear a dust mask and earplugs. Confine the dust to the room you are working in by hanging plastic drop cloths over all doorways and sealing the edges with masking tape.

Learn when and how to empty the dust-collection bags. To be safe, store the dust in a metal can until it can be disposed of.

APPLYING THE FINISH TO A FLOOR

Apply a stain or clear finish immediately after sanding a floor. In this way, you will avoid the possibility of an uneven finish by not allowing time for the grain of the wood to rise.

First of all, sweep and vacuum up all the dust, including that on windowsills and on the top of baseboards. Any dust and dirt that becomes stuck to the wet finish will create a bumpy appearance. At this stage, you should fill any nail holes or gouges in the floor. Fill these indentations with wood filler and then sand them even with the rest of the floor.

Painting wood floors If you are removing a clear finish, sand *(p.116)*, then sweep and vacuum up any dust. Apply either an oil-based or a water-based primer to the floor. Then use either a water-based floor paint or a deck paint for the final coats.

Painting concrete floors Although a concrete floor does not require sanding, you should clean the floor and fill cracks and dents with patching concrete. You can buy bags of premixed patching concrete at home-center and hardware stores. Then prime and seal the concrete with a masonry primer. Follow with paint that is made specially for concrete floors.

STAINING AND SEALING FLOORS

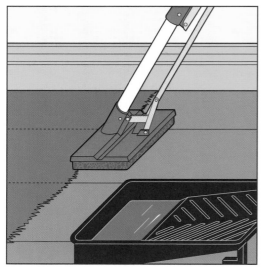

1 Applying wood stain
Use a roller, brush, or foam pad to apply the stain. Begin in the corner farthest from the exit and apply stain to a 4-by-4-foot or 5-by5-foot area. Once the stain has seeped into the wood *(p.87)*, wipe it up with clean cloths. Allow the floor to dry.

2 Applying a clear finish
If you are finishing with an oil-based polyurethane, buff the floor with a rotary buffing machine using fine steel wool. If finishing with a water-based urethane, use a buffing screen. Apply the finish around the perimeter of the room with a clean brush.

3 Apply at least two coats
Over the rest of the floor, follow the grain of the wood and apply the finish with a brush or a lamb's wool applicator. Buff with fine abrasives between each coat and clean up any dust. You should apply at least two coats of finish for proper protection.

PAINTING WOOD FLOORS

1 Paint along the edge
Start in the corner farthest from the exit. Use a 3-inch brush to paint a neat edge on the floor along the wall out from the corner in both directions. Paint an area about 5 feet along each wall.

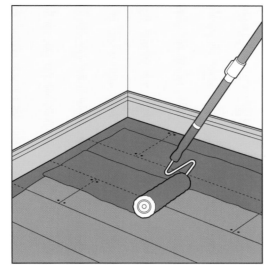

2 Paint along the boards
Use a roller and a roller extension. Lay on the paint in the direction of the floorboards within the border you have just painted. Make sure that the roller head contains a sufficient amount of paint.

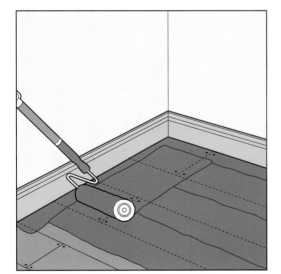

3 Paint across the boards
Without reloading the roller, paint across the boards, back over the area that you have just painted. The object of this is to make sure that the section is completely covered with paint.

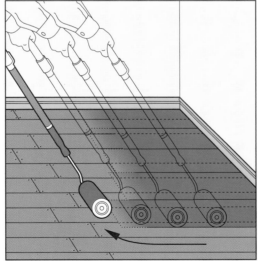

4 Paint the rest of the floor
Finish painting the entire floor by rolling paint along the wood grain. Feather the edges at the end of the section. Work across the narrowest dimension of the room first and be careful not to paint yourself into a corner.

PROFESSIONAL TIP

Painting floors is usually extremely uncomfortable, as you will have to work bending over and kneeling down. You can minimize bending by using a roller extension, but even then you will have to kneel to paint the floor borders with a brush. Wear knee pads (you can buy them in sporting-goods or gardening stores), or use an old piece of carpet or rigid-foam insulation board to kneel on.

PAINTING CONCRETE FLOORS

Lay on paint in a zigzag pattern
As for any floor, start in the corner and work in manageable sections. Lay on the paint in a zigzag pattern and then roll in a direction perpendicular to the wall for complete coverage.

Metal pipes and radiators

Many older homes have exposed metal pipes and radiators that can be painted to match the other colors in the room. The main difference between painting metal and painting wood surfaces is in the type of paint you use. Although most of the types of paint that are used for walls and woodwork can be used on metal too, it is best to use a paint that is specially formulated for metal. These products contain rust inhibitors and will protect the metal should the pipe be exposed to water because of a leak or condensation. Buy paint with a label that states that it is suitable for metal and contains rust inhibitors.

Dealing with hot pipes To avoid burning yourself, turn off the hot water when painting water pipes, and turn off the heat when working on heat pipes and radiators. Wait for the paint to dry thoroughly before turning the water or heat back on.

Painting pipes If the pipes butt against a wall, mask the wall for protection. It is also a good idea to lay a drop cloth on the floor under the pipe. You can use one cloth and move it along as you progress down the length of the pipe.

MATERIALS AND TOOLS

Metal primers
Metal paints
Wire brushes
Rollers and brushes (special shapes may be required for irregular surfaces)
Drop cloths
Paint mitt (optional)
Scouring pads
Paint sprayer (optional)

PREPARING AND PAINTING PIPES

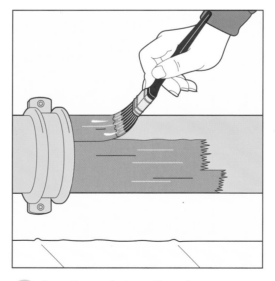

1 Prepare the pipes
Remove loose paint from metal pipes with a wire brush or steel wool. Avoid shaking the pipe loose from its mounting bracket by holding the pipe with one hand and brushing it with the other. Wipe the pipe with a damp cloth.

2 Lay the paint on the pipe
The pipe's size will determine which brush to use. Lay on the paint around the circumference of a small section of the pipe. Without reloading, smooth in even strokes down the length of the section. Move the drop cloth and continue to the next section.

USING A PAINTER'S MITT

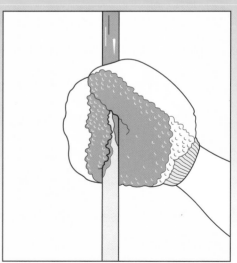

Dip the palm of the mitt in a paint tray and blot on the sloping edge of the tray. Grasp the pipe between the thumb and the rest of the mitt and slide the mitt along the pipe. Go back and forth a few times to ensure even coverage.

RADIATORS

Radiators present two main problems: they have hard-to-reach areas and they are usually set close to the wall, both of which make it difficult to paint the back of the radiator and the wall.

Cleaning radiators Make sure that the heat is switched off and the radiator is cool. Clean the radiator with warm water and soap to remove any dirt and grease. To remove stubborn stains, scour with a fiber scouring pad. Rinse the radiator and allow it to dry thoroughly.

Painting radiators Protect the floor under the radiator with a drop cloth. If you need to protect the wall behind the radiator, tape a drop cloth or plastic sheet onto the wall. Apply a water-based metal paint to the radiators if you wish to turn on the heat soon after painting it. The combination of oil-based paint and heat can produce unpleasant fumes until the paint cures completely. Paint the radiator with a brush or a paint sprayer to make sure it is completely covered. Remove or cover the radiator air vent before painting. This device allows air to escape from the heating system, and it will not be able to function if it is painted over.

PREPARING AND PAINTING RADIATORS

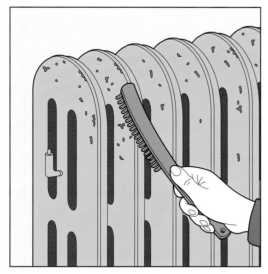

1 Preparing the radiator
Use a wire brush to remove loose paint. Then, using a long-handled brush for hard-to-reach areas, apply a metal primer to any bare spots and to radiators that have never been painted before.

2 Painting the radiator
You may have to use a number of different-size brushes to paint a radiator. Pads and minirollers on bendable handles can help you to reach the sections you would not be able to reach with a rigid-handle brush, roller, or pad.

USING A PAINT SPRAYER

Keep the tip of the paint sprayer perpendicular to the radiator as you move it from side to side. Protect the floor and the wall behind and on either side of the radiator by covering them with heavy paper or cardboard.

Masonry surfaces

Although they are usually left unfinished, brick, concrete-block, and poured-concrete surfaces can all be painted. Primers designed for masonry seal the porous surfaces of these materials and provide a good base for the masonry paint.

Preparing masonry Thorough preparation is as essential for achieving good results on masonry as it is on all surfaces. Dirt and grease should be removed with household detergent. If mildew is present, clean with a solution of one quart of chlorine bleach to three quarts of water. Allow the surface to dry.

Repair the walls by filling cracks. It may be necessary to replace mortar, a process known as repointing. Tackle only small repairs yourself; major repointing is best left to a professional. Make sure that you use the right type of mortar because modern mortar can damage old masonry. If you are in doubt about what to use, ask a professional who has worked on similar buildings.

Using a stiff-bristle brush Go over the entire wall, including grout and mortar joints, with a stiff-bristle brush dipped in cleaning solution. Rinse and allow to dry thoroughly. The brush will also remove loose paint, a help if the walls will be repainted.

MATERIALS AND TOOLS

Masonry primer
Masonry paint
Cleaning solutions
Stiff-bristle brush
Muriatic acid
Patching concrete or mortar
Trowel
Wire brush
Hammer and chisel
Pointing tool
Mortarboard
Brushes and rollers
Waterproofing compound

DEALING WITH EFFLORESCENCE

Efflorescence is a chalky, powdery residue that forms when salts leak out of the masonry. It will prevent paint from bonding to the surface properly and will cause the paint to peel a short time after it is applied.

To remove efflorescence, clean the area with a 10% solution of muriatic acid. Wear heavy rubber gloves, long sleeves, and goggles when using the acid. Apply it with a stiff-bristle brush. Rinse and allow to dry.

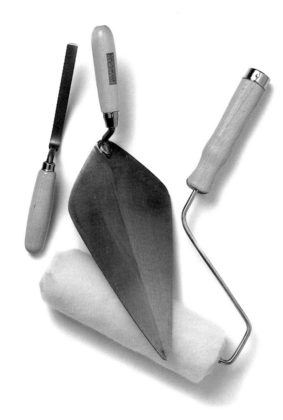

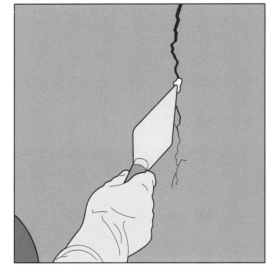

Patching a concrete wall
Use patching concrete for filling cracks in concrete walls. Mix the concrete according to the manufacturer's directions and apply with a trowel. Allow the area to dry and then scrub it with a wire brush.

REPAIRING AND PAINTING MORTAR AND MASONRY

1 Remove crumbling mortar
Use a hammer and a chisel to remove any crumbling mortar to a depth of about 1/2 inch. Wear safety glasses when removing the mortar.

2 Brush out the joint
Clean out the joint with a stiff-bristle brush. Be sure to remove all of the loose mortar. Mix new mortar and place enough to make the repair on a small board.

3 Mortar the open joint
Using the trowel, scrape mortar from the board into the open joint. Be as neat as possible but be sure that the joint is entirely filled. Use a pointing tool to smooth the joint. Remove any mortar that ends up on the face of the brick with a wire brush.

4 Apply the paint to the surface
Use a long-nap roller for applying paint to masonry surfaces. Lay the paint on in zigzags and then roll in the opposite direction for even coverage. Finish up with vertical strokes and proceed to the next section of the wall.

DAMPPROOFING BASEMENT WALLS

Minor seepage problems in basement walls can be eliminated by applying a waterproofing compound to the surface. Prepare the walls, then brush on waterproofing compound as directed on the can's label and allow to dry. Some cement-based products will require a few days to cure properly. Allow the first coat to dry completely before you apply a second coat. Waterproofing compounds can usually be covered with water-based paint.

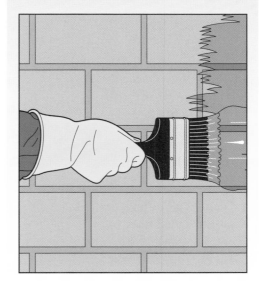

Apply waterproofing compound
Apply waterproofing compound with a large synthetic brush. Jab and pack the compound into all the joints and cracks. Allow it to dry before recoating.

Cleaning and storing equipment and materials properly is an important part of a paint job. If you have bought quality tools, following the cleanup procedures outlined in this chapter will help to prolong their life. You will also learn how to dispose of hazardous materials and to safely store paints and solvents for use on another paint job.

CHAPTER 9

CLEANUP, CARE, AND MAINTENANCE

Cleaning up

The steps you take for cleaning up will depend on which stage of the painting project you have reached. The procedure for cleaning tools each day during a paint job is not the same as that for cleaning up after you have completed the work.

During a painting project If you plan on continuing work the next day, there is no reason to store materials and tools. Just make sure that you pour the paint from paint buckets and roller trays back into the can. Then replace the lid and put the paint can out of the reach of children but close to where you will be working the next day. If you plan to use the room before resuming painting, roll up the drop cloths because they will be pushed out of position by normal foot traffic. But don't bother to remove painter's tape from windows and woodwork. Place brushes and rollers in plastic bags overnight. The aim is to keep your equipment in a convenient place and to leave the room ready for you to begin work without spending a long time setting up.

After a painting project If you have finished the project, cleanup should be much more thorough, and this final procedure is described in this chapter. An important part of the final cleanup involves putting the room back in order. Replace switch and electrical-outlet plates as well as light fixtures. Also, remove any painter's tape that is still in place. If you used water-based paint, it should be dry enough within a day of painting for you to remove the tape from window glass. For all cleanup, it's best to work at a large sink in the utility room. If you don't have a large sink, use a large bucket. After you have removed paint from brushes and rollers, allow the water to run for a few minutes to clear the drain of paint.

MATERIALS AND TOOLS

Buckets
Newspaper
Solvents
Rubber gloves
Spinning tool
Heavy brown paper
Roller tray
5-in-1 tool
Hammer
Containers with lids
Funnels

CLEANING AND STORING BRUSHES

With proper maintenance, a good-quality brush will last for years. The secret is to make sure that you remove all the paint from it after use. Start cleaning by running the brush across an old newspaper. This will remove much of the paint. Then treat the brushes with the appropriate solvent. For water-based paints, this means holding the brush under a stream of running water. Use mineral spirits as the solvent for oil-based paints. Help the solvent to reach deep into the bristles by flexing the bristles so that they fan out. Then dry the brush thoroughly and wrap the bristles before storing the brush. For long-term storage, hang the brush up so that the bristles do not support its weight.

CLEANING AND STORING ROLLER COVERS

A roller cover can soak up a lot of paint during the course of a project. Not only will the cover become saturated, but paint always seems to work its way inside the roller sleeve. To clean a roller cover, you will need to use a mineral-spirit solvent to remove oil-based paint. You may be able to remove water-based paint from a roller with your hand while holding the cover under running water.

CLEANING AND DRYING BRUSHES

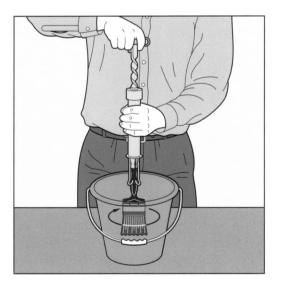

1 **Remove the paint**
Pour the correct solvent into a clean bucket. Wear gloves to put the brush in the solvent and rub the paint off the bristles; you may need a brush-cleaning comb. Dip a rag in the solvent and remove paint from the handle and ferrule of the brush.

2 **Dry the brush**
Wipe the cleaned brush on newspaper. Then wave it or spin it to remove excess paint and solvent. You can do this by hand or with a spinning tool. In either case, be sure to spin the brush so that the spray lands inside a bucket or trash can.

REMOVING PAINT FROM TOOLS AND YOURSELF

You may need to remove paint from the tools and yourself. Use a rag dipped in solvent to remove paint from tools. Make sure they are thoroughly dry before you store them.

Soap and water will remove water-based paint from your body. Shampoo should remove paint from your hair, but if it doesn't, comb paint out while your hair is wet.

Remove oil-based paint with a rag dipped in mineral spirits. Make sure that you wash with warm water after applying this solvent, as it may irritate your skin.

PROFESSIONAL TIP

Don't bother cleaning brushes or rollers if you plan on continuing the project the next day. Use the professional's timesaving trick of placing the equipment in plastic bags while it is still wet. The plastic will keep the paint damp. The following day, simply make a few practice passes and go to work. (*See chapter 2, p.27, for advice on how to refurbish old brushes.*)

WRAPPING AND STORING BRUSHES

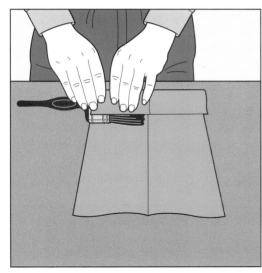

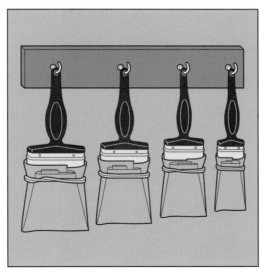

Wrap the brushes
1 When the brushes are clean and dry, wrap them in heavy brown paper or newspaper so that the bristles remain straight. Secure the paper with a rubber band or tie with string.

Store brushes properly
2 Store brushes by placing them on hooks so that their bristles hang free. You may have to drill holes in the handles. If you are storing a number of brushes, label the wrapping with the size of each brush.

CLEANING AND STORING ROLLERS

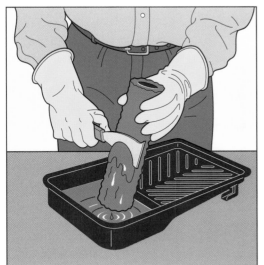

Clean rollers with solvent
1 Pour solvent into a cleaned-out roller tray and submerge the roller cover. Wear gloves and use a 5-in-1 tool to rub the paint out of the cover. When the cover is clean, squeeze it out and rinse it in clean solvent. Stand the cover on its end to dry.

Wrap rollers for storage
2 Wrap the rollers loosely in plastic or heavy brown paper. Secure the paper by twisting the edges of the wrapping.

REUSING TOOLS

You can reuse tools any number of times until they simply don't work anymore. Try a few practice passes with an old roller or brush before using it again. If it leaves brush or roller marks, or if it is not holding and dispensing the paint smoothly, get a new one.

If you unwrap a brush and there are still traces of paint on the bristles, or if the bristles come free when you give them a light tug, get rid of the brush. Many professional painters never reuse roller covers. They always use new covers for each project.

CLEANING PAINT BUCKETS

Clean small paint buckets by first pouring and brushing as much paint as possible back into the paint can. Next, use this bucket to clean brushes and other tools. Pour in solvent and use a brush to remove paint from the sides and bottom. Then clean the brush. Finally, rinse out the bucket and dry with clean towels.

STORING PAINT

Paint that is sealed and stored properly will, after a little stirring, be ready to use years later. At the end of a project, combine all of the leftover paint of the same color into as few cans as possible. If you cannot read the label because paint has dripped over it, write the color and sheen on a stick-on label and put it on the can lid.

Most paint labels provide information on storage. In general, place the paint in an area where it will not freeze and where children and pets can't get at it. A paint-storage cabinet that can be locked (*p.53*) is the best place to keep old paint.

Disposing of paint Small amounts of water-based paint can be poured into an absorbent material, such as shredded newspaper or cat litter, then placed in the trash. Recycle the rinsed-out cans.

Oil-based paint cannot be thrown out with the trash, as it is considered a hazardous substance. Make inquiries at your town maintenance department about how to dispose of the paint. It may be possible to donate leftover paint to charitable groups.

Disposing of solvents The solvents used for oil-based paints are hazardous and should be stored out of the reach of children. It is a good idea to recycle solvents for future use.

Seal the paint can
Remove paint from the groove on the lip of the can with a brush or rag. Place the original lid in position. Protect the lid with a rag while you use a hammer to seal it.

RECYCLING SOLVENTS

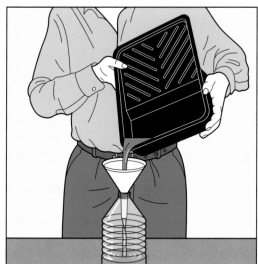

1 Pour solvent into a container
Pour the used solvent into a clean container. You may need a funnel. Close the lid tightly and leave the solvent for a few days to allow the paint particles to settle at the bottom of the container.

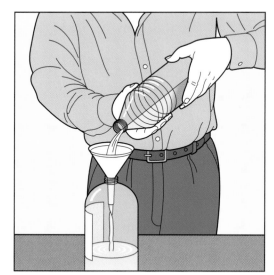

2 Decant the reusable solvent
When the used solvent has separated out, the clear, reusable liquid will settle over the paint particles. Carefully pour the clear liquid into another container with a lid and save the solvent for another painting project.

3 Dispose of the solvent residue
Add cat litter, sawdust, or any other absorbent material to the paint residue in the first container. Call your town maintenance department for information on how to dispose of unwanted solvents.

Care and maintenance

Regular cleaning will keep painted finishes looking like new. Surfaces with glossy sheens can be cleaned with soap and water, while duller surfaces should be dusted. Clean spots from flat or eggshell walls and ceilings with warm water. If that does not work, consult the manufacturer for instructions.

Keep a record of your paint jobs and the paint manufacturers' phone numbers so that you can get in touch with them, if needed. The record should also tell you the exact shade used during a project, how much paint the job required, and even how long it took to do the job. This is all valuable information when you decide to repaint the room.

Paint touch-ups You can repair any nicks and chips in a paint finish by touching up with the original paint. Use as small a brush as possible to apply the paint. If the touch-up dries differently from the original paint, you may have to repaint an entire section of surface. For example, if you make a repair, it may be necessary to repaint part of the wall or a section of woodwork so that the repair does not stand out.

Maintaining floors Use a dust mop or a vacuum with a wood-floor attachment to keep the surface of hard floors free of dirt. To remove stains, use a cleanser that is made for the type of surface finish that you applied. Restore the shine by buffing the surface with a lamb's wool pad.

When buffing no longer revives the floor, apply a new coat of finish. For polyurethanes, clean the floor and dull the existing finish with steel wool, a sanding screen, or sandpaper. Then apply the new finish in thin coats (*p.118*). Allow each coat to dry, as stated in the directions, before recoating.

PAINTING LOG

Here's what to keep for future reference:

- Dates of the painting project.
- Color samples and sheens for each room.
- How long the project took to complete.
- A record of the amount of paint you used, the number of coats you applied, and any repairs you made before painting.
- Manufacturers' phone numbers.
- All receipts.

PLASTIC CAN LIDS

You can buy plastic paint can lids for sealing open cans. Not only do the covers fit securely, but they can be reused. It is still necessary to remove paint from the can lip before sealing.

RECYCLING PAINT CANS

Paint cans are made from high-quality steel and should be recycled. Dispose of the paint safely (*p.128*). Then dry the cans and remove the lids. Aerosol-spray cans may also be recycled, but remove plastic caps first. Contact your local authority for information.

Glossary

ALKYD PAINTS
Also referred to as oil-based paints, although alkyds have actually replaced oils in paints. Mineral spirits and paint thinner are used as solvents for alkyd paints.

BALUSTERS
The vertical posts of a balustrade, which support the handrail.

BALUSTRADE
The components of a railing on a staircase which consists of the handrail, balusters, and newel post.

BOXING PAINT
Mixing together cans of paint of the same color, to ensure that there is a uniform color throughout the paint project.

BRUSH COMB
A tool which is used to remove paint from a brush.

CHAIR RAIL MOLDING
A strip of molding that is installed on a wall at about the same height as the back of a chair. In most cases, chair rail molding is a purely decorative feature.

CHEMICAL STRIPPER
A liquid which is used to remove paint from a surface.

COLOR WHEEL
A design device which shows the relationship of primary, secondary, and tertiary colors to one another. It can help you to choose and combine colors by noting the location of colors on the wheel.

COMPLEMENTARY COLORS
Colors which lie directly opposite one another on the color wheel.

COOL COLORS
Colors which contain elements of blue or green.

CROWN MOLDING
Molding which is installed where the top of a wall meets the ceiling.

CUTTING IN
Using a paintbrush to paint the edge where a wall meets the ceiling or woodwork. Cutting in ensures coverage right to the edge of walls or ceilings that are painted with a roller.

DECORATIVE FINISH
Any paint finish which results in an unusual design. The paint in decorative finishes does not dry to a solid color.

DEGLOSSER
A liquid which is applied to a shiny, glossy finish paint to make it appear more flat.

DRAGGING
A decorative paint finish which is achieved by pulling a brush through paint that has just been applied to surface and is still wet.

DRYWALL
Building material which consists of a gypsum core and paper facing.

DRYWALL JOINT COMPOUND
Material which is used to fill joints between sheets of drywall, and to make repairs in damaged drywall.

DUST MASK
A paper mask worn over the nose and mouth. This type of mask prevents the user from breathing in large particles of dust and dirt in the air.

EFFLORESCENCE
A chalky, powdery residue that is the result of salts leaking out of masonry and drying on the surface.

EGGSHELL
An intermediate and less intense level of sheen or glossiness.

FEATHERING
Brushing with the tips of the bristles on a brush; or a light touch when using a roller to blend two areas of paint.

LATEX PAINT
A broad term for water-based paints containing latex or acrylics in their formulations. Water is used as the solvent for latex paints.

LEAD PAINT
Paint which contains a high percentage of lead. As lead has been banned from use in paint you will only come across it if you have to remove old paint that contains lead.

PAINT PAD
A synthetic, sponge-like pad which is connected to a plastic handle. Pads are used to apply paint on narrow surfaces.

PAINTER'S TAPE
Tape which is used for purposes of masking objects while painting.

PLASTER
Cement-like material applied in layers and used in the construction of walls.

PLUMB LINE
A vertical line which is perfectly straight. The expression 'plumb line' also refers to the tool which is used to create a vertical line.

POLYURETHANE
A clear varnish which is applied as a protective coating, usually for wood.

RAGGING
A decorative finish which is achieved by applying paint with a rag.

RELATED COLORS
Colors which are located next to one another on the color wheel.

RESPIRATOR
Mask which screens out very small dust particles and purifies air as it is inhaled.

ROSIN PAPER
A heavy kraft paper which is used to cover and protect floors during a painting project.

SCAFFOLDING
In interior painting, this refers to a platform used for reaching ceilings. It is supported by ladders or sawhorses.

SHEEN
The level of glossiness of a paint when it is dry.

SOLVENT
A liquid which breaks down or dissolves other materials. Solvents keep paint liquid in consistency. They are used in the manufacture of paints, in cleanup, and removing paint.

SPACKLE
Material which is used to make repairs in drywall and plaster.

SPONGING
A decorative finish which is achieved by dabbing paint on a surface with a sponge.

TEXTURED PAINTS
Paint which contains additives and dries to a rough finish.

THINNING PAINT
The act of adding solvent to paint so that it flows easily.

TRISODIUM PHOSPHATE (TSP)
A highly concentrated cleaning liquid which leaves no soapy residue.

VOC
This stands for 'volatile organic compounds', a type of material that is used sparingly in paints because they can damage the lungs.

WALL LINER
Heavy paintable wallpaper which is used to cover cracks and other imperfections in walls.

WARM COLORS
Colors which have elements of yellow or red.

WET EDGE
The last section of paint which is applied to a surface. Painters keep a wet edge by applying new paint to a dry area, and then 'brushing back' to the wet edge.

Suppliers

Paints and Stains

Benjamin Moore & Company
51 Chestnut Ridge Road
Montvale, NJ 07645
800-826-2623

Deft, Inc.
17451 Von Karman Avenue
Irvine, CA 92714
800-544-3338

Duncan Enterprises
5673 E. Shields Avenue
Fresno, CA 93727
209-291-4444

Duron Paints and Wallcoverings
10406 Tucker Street
Beltsville, MD 20705
301-937-4700

Dutch Boy Paints
P.O. Box 6709
Cleveland, OH 44101-1709

The Flecto Company
1000 45th Street
Oakland, CA 94608
800-6-FLECTO

The Flood Company
P.O. Box 2535
Hudson, OH 44236-2535
800-321-3444

Glidden Company
92 5 Euclid Avenue
Cleveland, OH 44115
800-221-4100

Krylon Brands
31500 Solon Road
Solon, OH 44139
216-498-2300

Martin-Semour Paints
101 Prospect Avenue, NW
Cleveland, OH 44114

Minwax Company
10 Mountain View Road
Upper Saddle River, NJ 07645
800-526-0495

Muralo
148 East 5th Street
Bayonne, NJ 07002
800-631-3440

Parks Corporation
P.O. Box 5
Somerset, MA 02726
800-225-8543

Porter Paints
400 South 13th Street
Louisville, KY 40201-1439
502-588-9200

PPG Architectural Finishes
One PPG Place
Pittsburgh, PA 15272
412-434-3889

Pratt & Lambert
P.O. Box 22
Buffalo, NY 14240
800-289-7728

Red Devil, Inc.
2400 Vauxhall Road
Union, NJ 07083
908-688-6900

Rust-Oleum Corporation
11 Hawthorn Parkway
Vernon Hills, IL 60061
847-367-7700

Sherwin-Williams Company
101 Prospect Avenue, NW
Cleveland, OH 44115-1075
800-4-SHERWIN

United Coatings
980 North Michigan Avenue
Suite 1120
Chicago, IL 60611
312-944-5400

United Gilsonite Laboratories (UGL)
ZAR Products
P.O. Box 70
Scranton, PA 18501
800-UGL-LABS

Wm. Zinsser & Company
39 Belmont Drive
Somerset, NJ 08875-1285
908-469-8100

Wood-Kote Products
8000 Northeast 14th Place
Portland, OR 97211
800-843-8374

Tools, Equipment, and Repair Materials

3M
3M Center Building 223-4S-01
St. Paul, MN
612-733-1110
(paint removers and tapes)

Bondex International
3616 Scarlet Oak Boulevard
St. Louis, MO 63122
314-225-5001
(sealants, wood and wall repair)

Bondo Consumer Products
3700 Atlanta Industrial Parkway, NW
Atlanta, GA 30331
404-696-2730
(sealants, wood and wall repair)

Campbell Hausfield
100 Production Drive
Harrison, OH 45030
513-367-4811
(spray equipment)

Darworth Company
7405 Production Drive
Mentor, OH 44060
800-624-7767
(sealants and wood repair)

Daubert Coated Products
One Westbrook Corporate Center
Suite 1000
Westchester, IL 60153
800-634-1303
(tapes, wood and wall repair)

EZ Painter
4051 South Iowa Avenue
Milwaukee, WI 53207
800-558-3958
(paint pads)

Keller Ladders
3499 N.W. 53rd Street
Ft. Lauderdale, FL 33309
305-777-2060
(ladders)

Klean-Strip
P.O. Box 1879
Memphis, TN 38101
800-235-3546
(paint removers)

Plasti-Kote Company, Inc
1000 Lake Road
Medina, OH 44256
330-725-4511
(paint brushes)

Red Devil, Inc.
2400 Vauxhall Road
Union, NJ 07083
908-688-6900
(paint removers, sealants, and painting tools)

United States Gypsum Company
P.O. Box 806278
Chicago, IL 60680-4124
(drywall repairs)

Wagner Spray Tech Corporation
1770 Fernbrook Lane
Minneapolis, MN 55447
800-328-8251
(spray equipment)

Werner Ladders
93 Werner Road
Greenville, PA 16125
412-588-8600
(ladders)

Wm. Zinsser & Company
39 Belmont Drive
Somerset, NJ 08875-1285
908-469-8100
(paint removers and repairs)

Wooster Brush Company
604 Madison Avenue
Wooster, OH 44691
330-264-4440
(paint brushes)

Index

AUTHOR'S ACKNOWLEDGMENTS
Many paint manufacturers and professional associations that serve the industry provide valuable information for the do-it-yourself painter. Some useful suppliers' addresses are listed on page 132 and we referred to a number of them, especially Benjamin Moore & Company and Sherwin-Williams Company. The professional associations that we wish to thank include the Rohm and Haas Paint Quality Institute and the National Paint and Coatings Association for their kind help.

PUBLISHER'S ACKNOWLEDGMENTS
The publishers of this book wish to thank:–

Leyland Paint Stockists
335–337 Kings Road
London SW3 5EU
UK

Crucial Trading
4 St. Barnabas Street
Pimlico Green
London SW1
UK
(for supplying floor covering)

Photographic credits:

Werner Ladders p.32, p.55

Hiretech, Hire Technicians Group Ltd p.116

Geoff Dann: p.1, pp.2–3, pp.4–5, pp.8–9, p.18, pp.20–21, pp.22–31, pp.34–35, p.37, p.40, pp.42–48, pp.51–52, p.54, pp.56–58, p.60, p.63, p71, pp.75–80, p.82, p.88, p.95, pp.98–102, p.105, pp.108–109, p.115, p.118, pp.121–122, pp.124–125

Tim Imrie: p.11, pp.12–16

Matthew Ward: p.59